Islands in the Sound

Islands in the Sound

ALISON JOHNSON

Illustrations by John Busby

LONDON
VICTOR GOLLANCZ LTD
1989

Contents

Foreword

'*Tue. Aug. 29*   A young guillemot had caught a lovely red fish – very excited and noisy about it. Should he dive? Would he drop it? He dived, and didn't. Parent came to help, chick explained with much wing-flapping what had happened. We sailed out of sight so didn't see if he learned to deal with his catch or not.'

I keep summer notes on wildlife and sailing observations, unkindly categorised by my husband as the Country Diary of a Hebridean Bore. The entry above is fairly typical. I am aware that in those of a scientific bent it may provoke a reaction worse than boredom. *A lovely fish? Excited? Explained?* An unholy stench of anthropomorphism here!

I could be pedantic, and offer in defence that the term *anthropomorphism* was coined to denote the mistaken habit of casting God in the image of man; perhaps it does say something about human bigheadedness that our present use of the word implies that it is a greater blasphemy to allow other species common feelings and needs with ourselves. But I am not inclined to put up any defence where none should be needed. Anthropomorphism: in the form of the human: *animals* in the form of the human. So what? Humans *are* animals. Our limbs and vital organs, indeed much of the genetic material we inherit, are recognisably similar to those of other mammals, of birds or even of cockroaches. (So much so, apparently, that not all of us consider it shocking to replace a packed-in human heart with a piggy one. The pig might justifiably think different.) It would be very improbable indeed, so improbable I wonder how any rational person can entertain it, if, with all this common physical inheritance, we somehow shared no common emotional ground with 'them'. The division into 'them' and 'us' is usually arbitrary and mischievous: it's not so long since respectable thinkers who had no doubt at all that free white males had immortal souls could deny the same gift to women, blacks or slaves, depending on where they drew the line between 'them' and 'us'. It seems equally megalomaniac to deny our common emotional heritage with animals. We might *like* to get nearer the angels than they: but we have no more reason to expect success than the spoilt child who wants to grab the moon for her bedroom ceiling.

Of course 'anthropomorphism' really does carry some dangers, too. It is fatally easy to see members of other species as if they were infantile or imbecile humans, and to treat them in a degrading fashion as a result, ignoring their real needs and natures. It is the self-indulgently anthropomorphising tourist who pays to be photographed with a 'cuddly' baby chimp or lion cub on a Spanish holiday, without caring to find out that such creatures are abused, often drugged, and callously disposed of when they become too big to handle. It is the same wilful ignorance that enables us to see performing dolphins 'smiling', though 90% die in their first year of captivity.

But are we all so weak-minded that we can only escape the sentimental wallow by following the meagre signposts of scientific jargon? That path is certainly straight and narrow, but common sense may sometimes suggest that it does not always lead in the right direction; and natural common sense is as vital to our understanding of other animals as of our fellow humans. So is close personal attention, and a certain scepticism about old wives' tales: and here it is worth remembering that the eminent professor who has written a learned monograph on *Canis minimus idioticus* may be every bit as much of an old wife as that other one with the lilac perm who insists that her yappy lapdog understands every word she says. There is no substitute for using your own eyes and your own wits; and better do it quietly, or the creature you are watching will show only alarm and a clean pair of heels.

But back to my young guillemot: his actions plainly expressed excited delight, followed by consternation and a plea for help. The young blackheaded gull I witnessed a fortnight later, who paddled the mud adult-fashion, but who instead of fishing out the crustacea he had stirred up mewed and hunched in expectation of food from his recently absconded parents, was in even more of a recognisable quandary; though by the third day I watched him, he had learned to peck doubtfully between bouts of mewing. The young eagle I saw the same week, who shook off a pair of territorial hoodies with mature dash and dignity, then sat on a fencepost screeching for Mother was no less comprehensible. Our own young do not act very differently when they are first made to use a knife and fork or tie their own shoelaces.

I am not a professional biologist – if I were I should be unable to voice such heresies, even if I believed in them. But for many years now I have had a privilege which few professionals are granted, of living in daily contact with both wild and domesticated creatures of other species, in a locality of outstanding scenic beauty where they are at home. It can take a professional years of painstaking experiment to convince other professionals that hens prefer some environments to others – that hens are capable of preference at all. Odd that anyone ever doubted it: but two minutes' attention to our scruffy free-rangers going about their business would dispel any doubt. And where in scientific literature is it recorded that seals detest getting wet? Yet nearly every time we sail on an incoming tide we notice some pained-looking pinniped craning head and tail above the water encroaching on its skerry. (And knowing what it's like swimming in 11°C water, we sympathise.)

So I want to offer my observations of this wild, cold, lovely region where I and the creatures which so delight and fascinate me live. My existence is immeasurably more comfortable and secure than theirs: our house is weathertight, we can be warm and dry even in winter; and because humans, like squirrels, are food-hoarders, we have a full larder and are never hungry. We know no predators except the Inland Revenue, and the desperately long northern nights are cheered for us by claret and electric light. But outside the front door the wild world begins, with vast sky, roaring surf and a dizzying round of seasons that has nothing to do with Christmas dinner or bank holidays. Outside, everything is different and bigger. A bit out from land, half a mile, quarter of a mile, it is bigger still. Out there, the boat which seems so sturdy at the pier feels like little more than an extra layer of skin. In all that maze of water and rock and cloud, we are glad to greet as fellows any other flesh and blood, otter, tern or shag. Now we begin to guess how others live who don't live under a roof.

The Sound of Harris, between North Uist and Harris . . . is the only navigable channel through the Outer Hebrides, with the exception of the Sound of Barra. It is entered from south-eastward from Little Minch between Leac na Hoe and Renish Point . . . and from north-westward from the Atlantic between Shillay and Toe Head . . .

The bottom is chiefly fine white shelly sand, interspersed with rocks, which are invariably clothed with a reddish brown seaweed of great length, and easily visible when the sun is high . . .

A vessel might, in case of necessity, proceed through the Sound, or to a safe anchorage in it, but it is not advisable to attempt this without local knowledge, on account of the strong tidal streams and numerous shoals . . .

The tidal streams in the principal channels attain a rate of as much as 5 knots at springs. Elsewhere in the Sound of Harris they do not exceed 2½ knots. Vessels are recommended to make the passage at or near slack high water.

— *West Coast of Scotland Pilot*

Chapter 1

Sailing Around

We cut fairly eccentric figures among the working boatmen of the area. They scorn such contrivances as our buoyancy aids as unmanly, and besides there is a strong feeling that if it is the will of the Lord you should drown you had better go down promptly and quietly. Oddly enough, these criticisms don't seem to apply to radio communication: the smallest boat bristles with aerials and metal discs of which I cannot comprehend the workings. Electronic gadgetry, of course, is always and only manly. (If it were otherwise I would be able to understand how it worked – a point proved.) Since the Lord is masculine, craggy-faced, Gaelic-speaking and laconic, he presumably understands about radios too, so that's OK. Actually, I must admit to doubts about the point of tying these cumbersome red cushions round ourselves before putting to sea. The water temperature varies between 9° and 13°C: not conducive to survival, and what's the point of floating if you haven't survived? Rescue is fairly unlikely. The Coastguard inflatable stands on its trailer with one tube permanently deflated. Last time there was anyone to rescue, it took four hours to reach the scene, six miles away over a flat calm sea; perhaps they lost the pump or something. There is also a very sophisticated rescue helicopter based in Stornoway – or was. Last time *that* was called out, it crashed and sank.

Anyway, pointless or not, we wear buoyancy aids, dinghy sailor fashion. The boat in which we do most of our sightseeing (we have another, but it's the sort where you are too busy hanging on with your knees to see any sights) is not in fact a dinghy, but a Drascombe Lugger, a light eighteen-foot two-masted dayboat with an iron drop-keel. In spite of the folksy-sounding name, this is an ersatz design of a mere twenty years ago, with a clinker-look fibreglass hull and a handy hole in front of the traditional-seeming tail-spar to stick an outboard motor through. But in practice Drascombes need no excuse or apology. They are lovely sweet-natured boats to see and to handle, or at least our *Sand Eel* is. The flared prow, tan sails and varnished wooden spars have a veteran air, but the light weight and minimal draught are quite untraditional. The heavy metal centreplate provides all the necessary stability, whilst allowing dinghylike feats of daring in shallow water. A boat with a deep fixed keel would be far less manoeuvrable among the tidal reefs of the Sound; given reasonable weather, we can risk grounding if the plate is down, on the assumption that it will hit first then jump up leaving plenty of water under the boat. This works very well, provided no unfortunate is sitting on the centreplate case at the time, and that the helmsman manages to get the rudder up before that hits too, an uncertain business, since it has been bent so often it has to be wiggled out like an apple corer. Many of our dashing exploits have been ruined by my howls of agony as the iron plate rams up my backside, or by the sickening jar of the rudder's impact, followed by flapping sails and loud vituperation.

In fact, Drascombes were not designed for dashing exploits. They are intended as safe family pleasure boats which Dad can confidently sail without help while Mum attends to the baby and the lunch. There is no boom to whack tiny unsuspecting heads and plenty of locker space for the coolbag and the barbecue. The sail area is small, so that the boat hardly heels at all. 'This boat hardly heels at *all*,' Andrew often tells me, pounding into a Force 6 with water over the lee gunwale whilst our coccyxes bounce painfully on the weather one: Drascombes have raised sides to keep the tots safe and sitting out is consequently torture. As there are no toe-straps (whoever heard of Mum needing toestraps to butter the picnic rolls?) it is also precarious. However, although advertisements for Drascombes project a safe family image, they are capable of much sterner stuff. 'A boat like this one sailed two-thirds of the way round the world,' I have heard more than once as I ship green water down my neck and beg for toestraps.

I believe the skipper of that one gave up on the last third after pitchpoling three times. (Translator's note: *to pitchpole* – to capsize stern over bows, masts down, bottom up, and everybody out.) Even so, this and many similar ocean passages are remarkable tributes to the seakeeping qualities of these dauntless little boats.

We need all the talents *Sand Eel* possesses in our home waters, without ever touching the real Atlantic at all. We brought her from the less forbidding Cornish coast, all the way up the motorway behind a labouring Polo, with many halts and detours, because

Jet, our Labrador dog (a very unseaworthy fellow), had the horrors whenever he caught sight of the awful apparition behind us, and tried to save himself from its approaching bows by wriggling forward on to the driver's lap. Taking this as an evil omen, I droned premonitory gloom all the way home, and Jet agreed with every word. Andrew kept his temper, just.

He often lost it, the first season we sailed her; but he had reason to thank Mr Watkinson for designing a Dad-alone boat. Jet had immediately appointed himself first mate, but soon proved to be one of that unstable sort who used to be so common in the heyday of sail, given to alternate fits of manic enthusiasm and overwhelming melancholy. As we neared land (*any* land: there is a lot of it scattered about the Sound of Harris) elation would predominate. Singing a loud shanty, he would nudge figurehead-like into the bows, first a nose, then a broad chest, then two paws – at that stage, for his own good, I had to lunge forward and tackle him round the hindlegs. The skipper's language while we lay on our backs inextricably tangled in anchor chain and jibsheets was very unpleasant.

'Get your foot out of the mainsheet, can't you!'

'No I can't! I'm holding him with my knees.'

'Let him go, he'll be fine.'

'No he – help! Jet! *Come back!*'

With the maniac strength of ten, he had broken free of all the legs and arms and ropes and chains and was oozing over the weather side in pursuit of a passing razorbill.

'A capsize to windward is always worst,' remarked Andrew through gritted teeth, though not until I had lurched back centre with my black burden, provoking an alarming heel in the other direction.

'Tie him to the mast.'

'I can't do that! He wouldn't like it.'

'To the pump handle, then.'

'What if he falls out and strangles himself? What if the boat goes down and he's trapped?'

'Serve him bloody well right!'

'Oh, how can you ... he's smelt a seal! *Jet!*' This time I had enough presence of mind to wave a bar of chocolate. Jet ambled aft, but unfortunately attempted to go round the outside of the shrouds, an impossible feat for anything larger than a rat. Another flying tackle.

'Take the helm,' said Andrew grimly.

He put the mate in irons forthwith: but so heady were the odours of land and birds and seals that he scarcely seemed to notice. Uttering broken snatches of song, he lurched and rolled on his tether from weather to lee and back again, under and over helmsman and tiller, and . . .

'He's falling down the outboard well!'

'He's throttling himself!'

After that I tied him to my arm instead. We tried to keep at least 300 yards from land and preferably upwind of it. In the narrow channels available to us between the many islets and skerries, this was of doubtful value. We had to tack much too often and much too soon, in decreasing and desperate zigzags; and while the lugger can be put about very easily singlehanded, it is a different matter when the single hand is joined by four eager paws.

'Can't *you* help?'

'No . . . haven't a free hand.'

'Just get over to the other side and haul in the sheet.'

'Come on, Jet, over here – come *on*! . . . He's lying on the cleat.'

'Get him *off* then!'

And so on. My status as crew declined to that of nursemaid. Jet bore me down like a black furry albatross.

In his melancholy fit he was a little less volatile. If we headed, for respite, to more open waters, away from sweet-smelling land and familiar picnic places, the fear of the Lord and the watery wastes would fall on him. His boisterous song would change to a thin wavering lament, eerily keen above the hum of the freshening breeze and the hiss of the increasing swells. Sometimes a wave would spout up through the centreboard case, and the wail would change to gibbering shrieks of terror. He was a piteous sight: whiskers trembling, ears drooping, eyes and nose moist with reproach. And worse was to come. If the wind really got up, so that there was no option but for me to help, I would have to detach him and tie him to the pump handle. This was a terrible moment. As he felt the umbilical cord severing, he would give me one look of bottomless grief and betrayal. Had it really come to this? Had he not seen it, on the M6? Then with closed eyes and trembling limbs he would sink in the bottom of the boat to await the end. Henry Hudson, adrift with his young son in the Arctic wastes, could not have felt more guilty or more hopeless than we did then. We would turn as soon as possible for land, contorting ourselves to scrabble warm coverings or cheese sandwiches out of lee corners of the boat, swearing to renounce seafaring, sell the boat, anything, if only he would stop shivering and eat his nice sandwich. He would shiver more dramatically, even when we peeled off our own waterproofs and sweaters (steering with our feet and holding the sheets in our teeth the while) to add to his comfort; but he never refused his nice sandwich, and furthermore, at 299 yards from land, his mood would change and he would surge forward again, rolling his eyes and singing his merriest song: *Hurrah, we're homeward bound!*

And why, you may wonder, didn't we leave the brute at home? Really, I have no good answer to this, except that he wouldn't have liked it. But as the novelty wore off and age and stiffness increased, he became less insistent on going to sea. By his next sailing season, he would come only if Sarah was with us – not from doggy fidelity to his human sister, but to make sure she wasn't having some treat he might miss. By the following year, he inspected the picnic bag carefully before embarking, and would come for chocolate biscuits, but not, any more, for cheese sandwiches; and latterly he has hit on the happy system of picnicking in the car before the voyage, napping in the back seat during it, and decoding the fascinating odour network of Leverburgh pier after it. Nowadays, he only accompanies us on the water for camping trips, and when he does, he sports a natty blue and white canine lifejacket, because his poor old arthritic limbs can no longer support him in the water. What onlookers who despise the wearing of buoyancy even for humans think of this garment can be imagined.

It is disloyal to admit it, but it was a considerable relief when Jet retired from the sea. I discovered that I could learn to sail: that the difficulties of steering a straight course or raising the mainsail, though partly due to native incompetence, had been compounded by wearing seventy pounds of struggling Labrador slung from my right elbow. We saw far more wildlife, too. I think we had subsconsciously avoided it, in case it smelt enticing. It had certainly avoided us; there are few wild creatures which would not flee from the loud yodelling and yelping of Jet's best sea songs, except for grey seals, who loved them. Best of all, freed from the tyranny of the forced landing and the picnic bag (we could never disappoint him by not taking a picnic) we have more time just to sail where wind, tide and wildlife look most interesting. People often ask, 'Where did you go?' and the answer is usually, 'Oh, just sailed around.' The details are Sailing Bore talk, and would have any normal person looking glazed in five seconds; but we can usually add, 'We saw an otter,' or 'A baby seal was riding on its mother', or 'The terns are back', and most normal people realise it was a good experience.

There's another, less commendable reason for just sailing around: it's jolly difficult landing anywhere. Our area boasts only one slipway, at Leverburgh where we keep the boat. Even that is only usable above half tide, as the lower part has washed away. There are old jetties on two of the larger offshore islands, but apart from those it is a case of running the boat up on the sand and hoping the tide doesn't turn, or anchoring in the lee of the land and hoping the wind doesn't change. Drascombes are designed to make grounding on a sandy beach feasible. Imagine the footage, to Mendelssohn: the tan sails growing against the blue sea, the deserted shores of the Hebrid Isle beckoning. As the turquoise prow touches the lace-edge of foam between crystal water and golden sand, the jib furls at the touch of a nonchalant finger, the mainsail drops smooth as a theatre curtain. They leap ashore hand in hand, she in a clinging sarong, he in matching boxer shorts. Both are lithe and bronzed; if this is clean family fun, she might have a baby tucked into the back of her sarong, if not, flowers in her cleavage. She bends gracefully to pick up shells, he casts the anchor casually above high tide mark.

But life is not like that. However idyllic conditions appear, there always seems to be a brutal swell at the last moment, combining with a sudden onshore blast and a seized-up jib to force the boat broadside on, with a fearful jolt: and if you sit down that suddenly on the anchor you are glad to be wearing three pairs of trousers rather than boxer shorts. But after half an hour or so struggling and swearing and trying it again, a lucky lull may make it possible to get the anchor down and the boat secured to the shore by a running noose contrived from the ten leagues or so of rope Andrew keeps in all the lockers where the coolbags and barbecue should be. Even after that, it turns out someone has to keep anchor watch. He hovers between tidelines, pushing her out and pulling her in, shortening and lengthening the warps, grumbling about deteriorating weather and falling tide.

He has been proved right several times, of course. Responding for once to my impatient, 'Just beach on the sand, we're only going ashore for a minute,' he did just that on Ensay. The minute turned into a few minutes. We met the farmer, who was over for lambing, and chatted about the weather, and the lambs, and the boat. Idly, we watched the lazy tide recede, and talked about going soon. Suddenly, we had a strong feeling we ought to go at once. Too late! The keel was already firmly bedded in soft sand. The three of us heaved and strained, to no effect. Fortunately, the farmer's strong son appeared, with a big grin and a homesick sheepdog, who at once attempted to stow away, a little prematurely, I felt. With gigantic efforts, we got afloat, hurriedly jettisoned the disappointed sheepdog, and set the sails. Andrew was nobly restrained in his reproof; but I had learned my lesson. What if we had had to wait for the next tide? What would Jet have thought, abandoned in his car at the pier, without walk or dinner?

A rising tide is just as tricky. We were once caught out by one after a family picnic on Killegray. We had all been swimming, on a hot afternoon which had turned into a cool grey evening. Andrew was snorkelling in pursuit of a seal. Jet and Sarah had eaten the last of the food and had been dried as well as possible on our one damp towel. They were cold and hungry, Jet vociferously so. He had been prevented from joining in the seal chase, because in his swimming prime he rejoiced in retrieving snorkels, with dangerous effect. If he had not relieved his feelings by wrecking Sarah's sandcastle, stealing her chocolate biscuit, and sitting on the only towel, I might have noticed what was happening: the tide was creeping right up over the line led from *Sand Eel*'s bow to a rocky spit on shore, so that it would be impossible to pull her in to get aboard, because of the anchor out the stern. By the time Andrew came ashore, light-headed with cold and the wonder of his swimming companion, the boat sat in eight feet of water. We heaved on the bow line, but the anchor wouldn't budge. Jet howled in dismay, seeing his link with home bobbing out of reach on the cold grey ocean. The rest of us tried to be stoical, but nobody relished waiting in the chilly dusk for the tide to go out. Andrew bravely volunteered to dive for the anchor, and swam out watched by Jet, who looked hopefully for a snorkel poking up, but on seeing none, relapsed sulkily on his hunkers. When his master dived, he thought of leaping in to rescue him, but decided against it, in view of the cold. But when the anchor was freed and the boat began to move a little, an amazing thing happened: with a flash of enlightenment in pricked ears and gleaming eyes, Jet plunged in and swam not for the boat, but for the bow warp, biting and heaving on it before I could get near it. He lost it, dived for it, found it, lost it, disappeared beneath the water again. We all forgot about rescuing the boat in our rush to rescue Jet. When the shouting and splashing subsided, there he was, up on shore, bow warp in his teeth, hauling *Sand Eel* at dangerous speed straight for the rocks. Andrew interposed himself, and I sat on Jet. This true story raises interesting questions: is it possible that Jet, raised in a world of central heating and eiderdowns, behaved thus as a result of a genetic legacy from his ancestors in Labrador, who used to haul boats ashore through the freezing surf in just this manner? Or is atavistic memory something other than genetic coding? Or is he simply superbly intelligent?

Whatever the answer, it is much better not to be stranded by a rising tide; but even if tides would stay still, I doubt if the weather would. This is the problem about anchoring in a lee. We leave the boat snug in some placid high-sided cove, and spend half an hour peering into the still water after crabs and sea urchins. Then a saunter up to the top of whatever delightful little island it is reveals the horrible truth: the weather horizon has disappeared in an ominous steel-blue squall, the wind has risen two notches and shifted by 90°, is now against the current, and has whipped the strong tidal streams we must cross into a white-capped chop of unbelievable perpendicularity. So much for that relaxing spinnaker reach home.

These are the infallible results of going ashore. Much better just sail around!

Chapter 2

The Cat Died, the Pirates Died

S *tercorarius parasiticus* is a name suggestive of mean and
nasty habits, but seeing the bird itself in dashing falcon-like
flight you might credit it with a noble nature, for it is one of
the most beautiful and graceful of all seabirds. It comes in two
colourways, an all-over dramatic sooty brown, and an equally
striking dusky-backed, cream-bellied form. Both have wickedly
dark hook-tipped beaks and a tail rakishly ornamented with
pointed central feathers in the manner of an Edwardian villain's
waxed moustachios. These are the arctic skuas, and though there
is honour among the thieves themselves, to other birds they live
up to their Latin name, as shits, scum, lowest of the low, robbers
and parasites. Smaller and slighter than their cousins the bonxies,
they are no lesser pirates. Though they can and occasionally do
fish for themselves, and will also take small birds and mammals,
eggs and carrion, their preferred habit is to harass other fishing
birds till they drop their catch. Their most usual victims are terns,
but kittiwakes, gulls and even gannets are all good sport to skuas.
It is an astonishing but not an unusual sight to see a peregrine-sized
arctic skua buzzing a flying formation of five or six gannets – birds
twice its length, at three feet long, with six foot wingspan and
beaks like javelins. Gannets in flight are possessed of true military
loyalty, and no amount of strafing will induce them to break ranks,
either to retaliate or to flee: they can only flap on in their gorgeous
white and black uniforms, like stiff old generals at a dress parade
pelted with beer cans by bad boys. An arctic skua rarely makes a
gannet disgorge, but how it relishes the attempt!

A skua in aerial chase is capable not only of outpacing any
victim, but of stooping on it from above, jabbing from below, and
flipping its wings to knock it off balance, all at such high speed
that the bird under attack becomes disoriented and exhausted and
frequently coughs up its fish. Occasionally, though, even a small
tern succeeds in beating off its attacker, with the concentrated fury
of which terns are capable. Much more often, the outcome is
merely postponed, with the tussling group pelting backwards and
forwards across the water for several minutes, covering a consider-

able distance at top speed, and displaying strenuous tricks of evasion and pursuit. It would seem more efficient, in terms of energy expended, for the tern to give in with a shrug and try again, or for the skua to catch its own fish; but animals do not always act like perfectly calculated machines. Terns can be desperate, furious and stubborn, the skuas – well, it seems to be the case that skuas, like ravens, enjoy the fun, over and above the prospect of a free meal. Like ravens, too, pairs often co-operate in harassment, and when Blackbeard is joined by his moll, a victim has no chance at all. Arctic skua couples are as formidable in the chase as in defence of their nest-sites, where they are said to be only slightly less aggressive than the notorious great skua which has bloodied many an ornithological head.

Skuas, great and arctic, nest on open marshy moorland, usually near the sea, and convenient to a tern colony. Their British breeding stronghold is in Shetland, but there are small groups of one or both kinds in the Orkneys, the north of mainland Scotland, and a few islands of the west, but none in Harris. For years we were used to seeing skuas from August onwards, when they begin to disperse from their breeding areas and may spend a month or two pestering local birds before following the terns to the southern oceans, in the case of the smaller species, or to North Africa, in the case of the larger. Then one year we noticed a couple of arctic skuas on our first sail of the season, in late April. Their return passage in spring is not usually as leisurely as the autumn migration, and we were surprised to see them. During the next few weeks we saw several more birds, both dark and light phase. Then the terns arrived, and there were still arctic skuas around to annoy them. We began to suspect local breeding. One day as we approached the south end of Killegray we noticed a couple of skuas, a light and a dark, take off from the low-lying moorland there, fly over us in a languid but slightly menacing manner quite different from their rapid harrying flight, and re-alight on the moor. I was very excited: this must surely be where they were nesting. I demanded to be put ashore at once. Andrew expostulated about the falling tide, the rising wind, the guests waiting at home for dinner, but grudgingly agreed to attempt a landing in the narrow rock-infested channel between Killegray and Hestem, which dries at low tide.

After the usual interlude of swearing, bickering, lowering, hoisting and relowering sail, staving off with oar ends, and near loss of boat hook, I asked the usual question; why not use the engine? It got the usual rude answer, and I scrambled hastily ashore before I was made to walk the plank. 'Half an hour!' my testy skipper bellowed after me, returning to his grumpy manoeuvres with warp, ring and kedge.

I had no watch, and neither had he, and moreover I would rather be marooned than go home and cook dinner, and he knew it. Nevertheless as the wind was obviously getting up and I didn't relish shipwreck, I scoured the ground at high speed, leaping over disused peatbanks and splashing through bogs to the considerable indignation of all the oystercatchers, redshanks and common gulls. The skuas circled lazily overhead, looking insolent and cool. I quickly became very hot: the temperature on the water had been unpromising when we set out, and I was wearing a wetsuit under a woolly jumper and sailing smock. These garments together with my natural blubber soon combined to make me sweat, pant and stumble. The skuas, now joined by eight others, continued to look cool. Every time a bird alighted, I trotted hopefully up to it, expecting the threatening clicks and horizontal trajectory of territorial defence. But they simply took off at leisure from the most desirable lookout mounds, the most delectable crouches in the sphagnum and heather, and circled nonchalantly around the half square mile of promising, marshy, sea-girt, tern-bordered moorland. At last I found one nest and hoped hard it was an arctic skua's, as I had never seen their eggs; but the choice of site on an old grassed-over wall and the marking of the eggs looked depressingly like a blackback's, as indeed they proved to be. My will-o'-the-wisps led me back through the bog, and I slithered down to the boat muddy, perspiring, unzipped and unpopular. Knobbly rocks had appeared all around *Sand Eel*, and more knobbly rocks interspersed with largish waves between us and Jane's Tower.

Over the next two months, we checked the area several times, with always the same findings: eight to twelve skuas, flying frequently in pairs, and apparently occupying territories. We would see one or both birds perched on the prominent grassy cones which serve as lookout posts to several species of moor-nesting birds, growing more conical and brighter green with every year's accretion of guano. The skuas had probably adopted posts used by black-backs at other times. On each occasion, the same lookouts were being used, and from the positioning of two dark birds, two light birds, or a light and a dark together, it looked very much as if particular pairs were remaining in preferred areas. But they showed no interest in seeing us off, and we found no nests, and later, no young.

The following year the skuas were back. My diary reads: 'Usual abortive landing in freshening wind but at least a rising tide.' In view of the rising tide, I tramped the area more thoroughly than ever, and found the same number of birds as in the previous year occupying the same lookout posts. But this time they seemed to have wakened up. Pairs were defending their territories against neighbours with vigour, leaping and flapping on the lookouts and pursuing in the air with determination, continually emitting their rapid "kee-ow ow, kee-ow ow", on a rising inflection, rather like a police siren. But in spite of constant squabbling amongst themselves, they took very little notice of me. No nests yet, I thought, but there definitely will be soon.

I should explain that we very rarely blunder about looking for birds' nests; in fact, we usually avoid them if we know they are there. If the skuas had been, say, red-necked phalaropes, which would be another breeding 'first' for our locality, we would have left them undisturbed and hoped to see fledged young later to prove our guess. But since skuas are eminently capable of looking after themselves, I didn't feel too guilty about searching their territories. However, I had more compunction about the anxious oystercatchers I was flushing as I walked up from our customary landing place at the south end, particularly as there was also a small colony of blackbacks in the area who would be delighted to gobble up a few succulent wader chicks. So on our next visit a few weeks later, we landed at a small mud creek on the east side of the skuas' moor, hidden by rising ground from the tern colony: we certainly didn't want to bother the much-harried terns. The drier part of the moor which I had to cross to reach the skuas by this route held a small enclave of herring gulls and another of common gulls. They were extremely nervous and defensive: one herring gull swooped round my ears again and again, not actually striking, but close enough for me to feel the whirring blast of air through its primaries and spread tail as it braked and shot up again for a new attack. Gulls very rarely behave like that, relying as they do on loud threats to drive off intruders. Presumably having skuas next door had driven these to desperation. Perhaps, I thought, I had missed the skuas' nests somehow last time, and they were actually already feeding young. But no; they were undoubtedly stuffing their own faces with gull eggs and chicks, but they hadn't the excuse of feeding the family. They were there as before, paired and territorial, a Lord and Lady Macbeth at every green watch-tower, loud in defiant speech and quick in violence with their neighbours; but no chicks, not even nests.

I tried once more, at the end of June, when even the tardiest skua should at least have been sitting on eggs. It was the same story, birds behaving territorially, but without the intensity of aggression which eggs or chicks should evoke. The dive-bombing herring gull was as angry as ever, though, so presumably the skuas hadn't yet devoured all its offspring.

Why these paired skuas in possession of perfectly suitable territories have not bred, or even apparently attempted to breed, remains a puzzle. It is possible they are young pioneering birds, though they have certainly worn adult plumage for at least two summers, assuming they are the same birds, which seems likely. It is known that arctic skuas don't breed till about four years of age, and it may be that like several other long-lived species they pair off and take up territories well before actually mating, though I have not been able to ascertain this. Next year may answer that.

Another possibility is that something about the food supply is wrong for feeding young skuas, and that the adults won't breed until conditions appear right. Killegray provides insects and other birds' chicks and eggs, but it may be that the most suitable food for the young is the same as for young terns, auks and red-throated divers – juvenile sand-eels. It seems unlikely that omnivorous skuas would be so finicking as not even to attempt breeding because of scarcity of a particular food, but it is just possible, say, if these are young birds who require that same easily-assimilable high protein food to bring the female into laying condition for the first time.

The summer presence of these birds in a new area is probably a sign of scarce resources further north; certainly it is not because the terns which they follow are increasing locally, for the reverse is true. The seabirds of the Western Isles have not suffered anything like the crashes of the last few years in Shetland, but there have been ominous signs. In 1986, the large colony of arctic and common terns on Scarista beach suddenly deserted before fledging. At the time we put this down to human disturbance, which had been considerable, and since someone had ridden a motorbike through the middle of the colony at the critical hatching period, this may in fact have been the reason. But against this, in the following year, the small roadside colony two miles away increased slightly, although it is next door to a busy sheep fank and is frequently infested by tourists 'trying to get a picture of the terns' by having their gesticulating spouses leap around in the middle of the nesting area. The terns on this packed little oblong of grass are understandably permanently frantic, but so far numbers have not declined. We assumed that a few of the beach colony had moved into the fank colony, but have no proof of it. In 1988, a few pairs of arctic terns returned to the beach, but the total population of this western side of Harris is certainly less than half what it was two years ago and for years before that. Since the birds which used the beach up to 1986 left during nesting, rather than just not reappearing at the beginning of the season, we must assume that their problems are local, and not connected in this case with disasters on migration. It was suggested at the time that they might have been bothered by a common gull colony half a mile away, but this seems exceedingly unlikely, since the fank colony nests within yards of a dozen pairs of common gulls; and on several islands we have seen mixed colonies in which there is frequent bickering, and maybe some predation, but the terns stay put. The remaining possible cause of desertion is, of course, lack of the right size of sand-eel to get the adults fit for breeding and to feed the young, and this may well be what drove our terns away. Interestingly enough, the few pairs of little terns which always nested on the outskirts of that colony continue to do so; in fact, they increased by at least two pairs. This could be due to slightly different feeding habits, as they take proportionately more marine worms, for which we often see them fishing in the warm wormy shallows where Scarista sands flare out towards the Northton saltmarsh.

Lack of food is almost certainly the reason for the next sad tern story. Early in 1988, as in previous years, the small island of Sleicham hosted a thriving colony of arctic terns. Certainly, they had unpleasant neighbours – common, herring and blackbacked gulls, each densely populating a discrete area of the island. The disposition of the various species on the island had not changed, the island was not grazed and therefore not trampled, and as far as we could gather there had been no human disturbance. Yet by late June, before fledging could possibly have taken place, all the terns had gone except for three adults. In the fortnight following we noticed that sites on Ensay and on Hestem which had been used in previous years by arctic terns had none, but as we had not checked them earlier, we could not tell whether this was due to general decline of numbers, removal elsewhere, early fledging or desertion. The other half dozen colonies in our part of the Sound were all occupied as usual, but in two numbers looked down at a cursory estimate, and none looked as if they had expanded.

Skuas aren't good for terns, but what's bad for terns is ultimately bad for skuas. If terns are locally in decline, a new population of arctic skuas will do them some damage in the short term; but if the terns continue to fade away, it will not be long before the skuas follow them. This has already happened in Shetland, where very few arctic skuas survived to fledging in 1988, and where even the famous bonxies of Foula reared only one chick per ten pairs. Such drastic decline among birds capable of eating almost anything (including their nephews and nieces) does seem to indicate that the sand-eels which they force kittiwakes, puffins, and particularly terns to disgorge are important to the feeding of the young.

So the future looks uncertain for the pirates of Killegray. Splendid as they are, I shan't be too sorry if they don't settle: our local terns face enough uncertain pressures without them. Summer hasn't sounded like summer since the clamouring terns left our beach, and it will be a sad year, if it comes, when their excitable voices are silenced among the green islands of the Sound.

The cat died, the pirates died: thus the five-year-old author of *The Pirate's Tale* disposed unsentimentally of all her characters on the last page. She had no further use for them, so that was that. That may soon be that for *Stercorarius parasiticus*, the least numerous breeding seabird in the British Isles, not hanged in chains for swashbuckling villainy, but ignominiously starved for want of plunder.

Chapter 3

Swift Currents, Still Lagoons

S tretching south of Ensay is a three-mile curve of low skerries ending in the decisive conical bulk of Dunaarin, which dominates the entrance to the deeper waters of the Minch. From Killegray, another jumble of reefs and islets straggles southwards. In the gap between Ensay and Killegray, five-knot tides rip through Caolas Skaari and sweep the sandy bottom clean and deep in a narrow channel between the two lines of rock. On the Admiralty chart, the area is neatly defined: separate blobs of intertidal sage green in two pools of shallow water blue, with a slender but reassuring stripe of deep water white pointing to the open sea. In actuality, except at dead low water, the relative dispositions of shallows and reefs is always doubtful. The 'reddish brown seaweed of a great length, easily visible when the sun is high', though a useful clue when the sun *is* high, is not to be trusted when conditions are murky. 'Only navigable by small craft with local knowledge,' concludes the *Pilot*, of this channel.

Local knowledge is difficult stuff to pass on. The Sound is such a jigsaw of reefs that local knowledge verbally conveyed has run into ten minutes' solid information before you have enough to take you safely out of harbour. Landfalls on the larger islands can be described by reference to locally used bearings, as can hazards near or in what pass for channels; but if, like us, you simply want to explore as much rock and water as possible, the way to acquire knowledge is by hit and miss, quite often hit: hits stick in the memory more usefully. The slowing down or total halt consequent on impact offers a chance to look around and think, 'Ah yes, must remember next time not to let the telegraph pole out of line with the end of the gents' loo on the pier', or 'Should have kept Campbell's shed directly below the water tower.' Next time, of course, there will be arguments as to whether the landmarks were to be kept *in* line or *out* of line; but a second grounding usually establishes that once and for all.

This sort of trial and error is only possible in pleasant weather, when the worst punishment to be expected is broad grins lining the Berneray ferry as it sweeps sensibly through the channel. In a brisk wind or with a swell running, the outcome might be worse than embarrassing; but if conditions look promising, we often cut across the recognised channels and into the maze of weed and reefs where no one else has any reason to go. The Sound as a whole has very little boat traffic: one might see, perhaps, three or four one- and two-man fishing craft, the *Endeavour of Berneray* ferrying cheerfully between North Uist and Harris, a couple of trawlers four miles away in the Minch, a summer yacht motoring through cautiously at slack high water. But among the reefs, even this slight traffic fades from sight and hearing, hidden and muffled by the low walls of rock on all sides. The swift currents of the channels have their own noises, a swish and smack against the boat, and a movement of waves that draws the eye into the distance, and these too are left behind, as the tidal streams divide to run unimpeded either side of the area of reefs and islets. The wind appears to drop, deflecting, like the current, from the low broken humps and ribs of rock. The water is smooth and still, and clear to the bottom. It is a magical, pristine world, where you unconsciously lower your voice to accommodate the quiet, where everything seems close enough to touch, from the otter on the skerry to the velvet crab on the seabed; where other senses become so delightfully acute that you feel you *are* touching, rather than merely hearing or seeing.

Here is 'the reddish brown weed of a great length': tangle forests. Moored south of Killegray one pearly afternoon, I crouched over the chart, trying to put names to what I was seeing: Sgeir Fhadbhig, Kylie, Bodha Breac, Hachla Sgeir, Bodha Dubh Iain Mhic Coinnaich. But the names were more disorienting than helpful: this was not land, no recognisable bulks or outlines, only a wide circle of glistening kelp, softening the contours of rock above water and concealing the depth of what was below. Outside the ring, a distant lobster boat chugged through the familiar mid-channel chop, among the mundane profiles of land-tinted islands; inside was a still lagoon, so hushed that the kelp fronds barely stirred in the water. Time moved gently to suit the slow questing feelers of the little winkles grazing the weed, soft grey-green bodies gloriously shelled in bright yellow, scarlet or humbug stripes. Some of them were so tiny as to be invisible at first; but all were poking out feelers, all brilliantly coloured against the rich brown weed. There were some tops among them, far more pearled and striped in life than the dead shells suggest, and a sea urchin, delicately flushed with pink and lilac, and haloed by its waving semi-transparent tube-feet. The live animal shimmers with fluid movement and luminous tints, quite unlike the static, brittle empty test one finds washed up on the beach.

Watching the urchin's rippling on-the-spot dance, I wished it would propel itself sideways under a weed-frond, away from the rapacious eyes of old Baba Yaga: blackbacks are particularly keen on urchins, and there were several diving and disputing on the next-along skerry. But the bird flying over was carrying a razor fish, and heading south-east. This explained a long-standing mystery: on Langay, which is a rather featureless island about two miles south of where we were moored, we had been puzzled by the numerous razor shells, since it is a steep-to, rockbound island without the shallow sandy bottom necessary to support these molluscs. Now we watched the birds disappear speedily with their catch; they must, at least sometimes, carry it all the way home before alighting to eat, ignoring other apparently suitable perches in between. It was obvious from the positions we had found the shells on Langay – neither near the breeding ground, nor always in the breeding season – that they fed there out of preference, not simply because they were bringing food to the nest. We had known gulls have favourite eating places, often low promontories of turf or smooth rock, which you may find littered with crab, urchin or mollusc shells, but it was a surprise to find that the dining room might be so far from the larder: we had always assumed the eating area was chosen for proximity to available food stocks.

On the sandy bottom inside the edge of the tangle, shore and velvet crabs scuttled from one clump of weed to the next, leaving clear 'footprints' in the sand, which was strewn with razor shells, though we saw no live ones. Blackbacks' eyes are sharper, capable of picking out the creature's siphon, which is all that shows. Clumps of bright green sea lettuce lolled on the still seabed like blown roses. From scattered pebbles on the bottom, bootlace weed and saw-wrack trailed languidly upright, diffusing an oily haze from the swollen fruiting tips, and flounced with fluffy yellow tufts of *Leptosiphon pusillus*; but where a wayward shaft of current forced through a gap in the reef, the water chilled and livened, and the vegetation changed abruptly to eel-grass, streaming not upwards but horizontally. This is not a seaweed but a rooting plant, which can bend to swift currents but must have shallow water to admit sunlight and soft ground to root in. Though usually a plant of estuaries, it is abundant here where the current sweeps the sandy shallows clear, allowing plenty of light. Under its more imposing name of *zostera*, it is highly regarded by biologists for the invertebrate creatures it encourages. Even as eel-grass, it is special for its visual attractiveness: one of the most exquisite water patterns is the leaf-green blades streaming with the current against white sand, crossed at a slight diagonal by flickering broken lines of silver – a shoal of sand-eels, casting shifting flecks of viridian shadow on the bottom in a three-dimensional checkerwork of pure abstract beauty.

We crossed the clean colours of the *zostera* bed and nosed in to the other side of the lagoon, a yet more enclosed and more placid basin bounded outside the reef by the sprawl of islets south of Killegray. The water here was warm and fertile, cloudy with seaweed mucilage, plankton and mud. Large blue winkles grazed enormous fronds of crinkled yellowish *laminaria*; when we parted the weed, we found groups of pale flaccid snakelocks anemone, and the boulders below were cushioned with sponges grown to unusual size and squashiness in the rich water. The rock crevices above low-tide mark glistened with well-fed beadlet anemones. A drowsy afternoon fragrance drifted from ungrazed Eliean na Ciardach, where angelica and mayweed softened the flotsam of old plastic bottles and bleached driftwood scattered below its lichened boulders – marvellously lichened, with bold whorls of black, scales of hot orange, beards of delicate ice green: the colours and textures of land, though of land on the edge of the sea. A bumblebee buzzed past our ears, heavy with pollen, heading across the lagoon for home on some further island. A group of eiders slipped into the water and paddled circumspectly away, a female followed by three dark fluffy ducklings, with another female bringing up the rear. In our immediate area, eiders usually nest solitarily, yet it is very common to see an 'auntie' with a mother and brood.

She might literally be an aunt or an elder sister, or perhaps a female who has failed to breed herself through youth, age or infertility.

Engaging though the ducklings were, scuttling over tangle and arrowing through the open water, we had hopes of seeing still more charming babies that day. It was mid-June, the right time of year. We cut quietly through the water. The barely perceptible breeze would have been quite inadequate if there had been the slightest wave, but the surface scarcely ruffled. We were reluctant to use the noisy engine, which not only frightens birds and animals away, but blunts one's awareness of their presence by obliterating the useful hints of sound – a splash, a wingbeat, a scrabble. We glided slowly in and out of the reefs, within touching distance of the weed-draped rocks, sitting very still and almost holding our breath for fear of grounding, and also because of the enchanted peace of these kind life-nurturing waters.

A sudden small commotion in the water, and a little round seal face not ten feet away – it was the infant we had hoped to see, the midsummer innocent. He liked us, he came closer – mother swiped him from behind, and both disappeared in a flurry of bubbly ripples. He bobbed up again, curious as before, but this time the mother got underneath him, and he flipped onto her shoulders and rode merrily away, distracted from his interest in us by the new game. They soon dived, but once at a safe distance, the mother relaxed, and they reappeared, bobbing and rolling.

The first common seal pup of the year, at least the first we had seen. Two plump seal cows, we now noticed, lay near us on a high skerry. They turned heads to watch us, but were presumably too heavily pregnant for the effort of flopping down to the water to seem worth while. One of them kept stretching her tail end up uneasily. Births might very well take place before the next high tide. Common seals, unlike greys, pup in the intertidal area. Elswhere, as in the Wash, they prefer sandbanks, but in the Northern and Western Isles they make use of offshore rocks and reefs. The sheltered bays and pools formed by such features make safe havens for the babies, who are afloat at the first high tide after birth, and soon swim and play confidently like the cheerful infant we had just been watching. They are born precociously developed, proportion-ately heavy (about twenty-five pounds, one-tenth the weight of a large adult) having already shed the baby white coat in the womb, and with large strong hind flippers to facilitate swimming. Mother and baby stay together for the four to six weeks of suckling, and possibly for longer. The babies grow quickly on rich milk, and are lively and playful. In the sheltered nursery waters, after the pups are a few weeks old, you may see several playing together, bursting through the weed which covers the surface of half-tide pools, while the mothers doze on the rocks, freed for a while from the little pests' mischievous attentions.

Well pleased with our sighting, we turned into the miniature tide-rip between Hestem and Vacam, four feet deep and not much wider, bubbling and rippling like a mountain burn past tangle filled with tiny crabs eager for the prizes of the incoming tide. We went ashore on Vacam to count breeding birds, but there weren't any; even the blackbacks of the previous year had been forced out by the presence of grazing sheep. Half a dozen had been marooned there and left to devastate the vegetation, so that the lush fragrant herbage found over the narrow channel on ungrazed Eilean na Ciardach had been replaced by impoverished monotone dull green, smelling only of the sheep droppings which covered it. The sheep looked as depressed as the vegetation. Neighbouring Hestem was no better: there is a low-tide causeway between the two islands, from the days when areas of nourishing seasonal growth were kept as summer pastures. A couple of young girls or an old granny might have camped out here with a few cows between mid-May and mid-July, visited by a boat every day or so to collect the precious dairy foods which were the staples of the Highland diet. The place would never have been grazed like this then: the soil's fertility was too valuable to squander on lazy sheep management. We found the remains of the milkmaids' tiny drystone bothy, filling half the breadth of the diminutive island. Lengthways, it seems a bigger place, and across shallow channels further thin low spines of land show, bare, grassed or flowered, or brown and gleaming with seaweed, a tranquil summer patchwork spread between the familiar profiles of higher land, Roneval, Renish Point, Dunaarin, Leac na Hoe. Not much wonder the shieling days were accounted the best of the year and the best of life: at least when the midges weren't out.

Vacam's pasture is denuded, but the intertidal mud which splits it across into two separate high tide islets is as rich as plum pudding. Ringed plover and dunlin were feeding busily as a border of scummy water began to encroach, sending up a bubble for every wormhole it filled. This mud is always strewn with large shells — scallops, quahogs, razorshells and ottershells, graded out by the current which carries smaller lighter shells further afield.

We had a last quiet look at the heavy cow seal, in case a pup might have made its appearance, but she was still straining her tail restlessly. I felt sorry, that day, that if I met her with her pup a fortnight later, I would not recognise her. Common seals look almost uniformly black in the water, and one round head is much like another.

In fact, it is difficult without a lot of experience even to tell a common from a grey when all you see is a wet moving head at a distance. On the whole, common seals are commoner on the east side of Britain than on the west, grey seals the other way about, but in north-west Scotland you are as likely to see one as the other. The head shape is diagnostic: the common seal has a shorter, rounder head with a more snub nose in profile, and full face its nostrils are seen to be at an acute angle to each other, forming a V. The grey has a longer nose without a forehead, and nostrils almost parallel to each other. However, the distinctions are not as easy for the inexperienced as they sound, for while a mature grey bull has a most imposing and unmistakably Roman conk, younger animals are often prettily retroussé, and nostrils are not always distinguishable. Coloration is some help, as an animal noticeably lighter underneath is almost certainly a grey. Males are darker than females, but even they often show well-highlighted multiple chins, and anyway their enormous size makes them easy to spot. As you get to know seals, typical movements offer clues, too. A seal 'bottling' (reaching a long nose up in the air and leaning blissfully backwards) is almost always a grey, whereas an animal swimming sideways on but with head turned full face is usually a common. Grey seals in mature blubber cannot turn their necks that easily, indeed a seal with a recognisable neck is unlikely to be a grey: greys feature mayorial *embonpoint*. There is something sublimely relaxed and self-satisfied about the normal progress of a grey seal through the water, whereas commons often seem rather anxious and hurried near human presence. Once they are ashore, size is a good guide, since greys are much larger, cows up to six feet and 300 pounds, bulls up to eight feet and 500 pounds, as against four and six feet with rather less weight in proportion for commons. Noise is also an identifying feature: an unearthly choir on a distant reef must be greys, as commons only growl. As they dry off on their rock perches colour is indicative: greys usually look silvery grey when dry, whereas commons can be anything between creamy white and boot black, with various shades of brown, yellow-grey and buff predominating. Since the two species haul out separately (though they may use the same reefs on different days) a basking group can be identified from a distance by colour alone.

I remember one delightful group of common seals we saw on Coddem, where there is another lagoon much favoured by otters and seals with young. This picturesque family consisted of an almost terracotta male with one small buff and another larger donkey-brown female, and a chocolatey-dark pup. I have called them a family, as that is the impression we got from seeing the same sociable grouping on several occasions during the first half of July. The male was alert, with watchful eyes peering above fine whiskers, the females quite relaxed. The smaller of the two could have been an immature from a previous year, or a young wife late in giving birth. But scientific literature on the common seal gives no substance for their classification as a family unit. Young animals are assumed to part from their mothers after weaning at the age of six weeks or so, and males have only been observed keeping company with females during the mating season in late summer, and sometimes in bouts of erotic play in spring, of which the purpose is unknown since it does not usually lead to coition. The biologists who are so put out by the seals' spring frolics are presumably not so puritanical about the purpose of their own lovemaking; but still there is plenty to suggest that our nuclear family should not have been sitting on Coddem in early July in domestic tranquillity. Such expert evidence as there is can offer no interpretation: yet to see the same individuals together day after day does not suggest accidental grouping. The puzzle would not have appeared to be one, without the unusual circumstance of being able to recognise individuals, which is very difficult except when they are dry, and probably impossible even then if large numbers of seals are being observed together. But it has to be faced that without such individual recognition, analysis of social relationships must remain hazy. It cannot be proved that young common seals stay with their mothers after weaning: nor can it be proved that they don't, unless individuals are clearly recognisable. There is no proof that seals are other than promiscuous: but if every male looks like Jack to us and every female like Jill, how are we to know they are not actually lifelong monogamous partners? The one conclusion is no more verifiable than the other unless individual animals can be recognised. 'Scientific' deductions based on insufficient evidence are simply a matter of taste, in the end. My taste would lead me to infer that, in this particular group, the male was indeed the donkey-brown female's husband, at least for that year. He would keep her company through the summer and mate with her in September, and next year's pup, though not necessarily the chocolate-brown infant he was tolerating at the moment, would be his. His protective influence, such as it was, extended to his mate's previous offspring, the buff virgin cow, whom he might or might not impregnate as well later in the year.

Well, there is absolutely nothing to prove it. There is absolutely nothing to disprove it, either. There is evidence in many other social species (red deer and chimpanzees, to name two disparate examples) that mothers and offspring retain a special relationship well past weaning, and in the case of daughters, past adolescence too. The two female seals, like the eider mother and 'auntie', were at least as likely to be blood relations as not. As for the not-so-promiscuous male: perhaps the spring frolics sometimes result in pairing off, though mating proper is a later business; perhaps the virgin cow, sighted at the spring carnival, was the attractant who kept the bull in tow; perhaps the solemn whiskered male and the dowdy brown female had been married for ten years. Who knows?

One day someone may carry out a lengthy study of common seals using radio transmitters or other gadgetry to keep track of individuals, and we may learn more about their social relationships.

Until then, the gaps can only be filled with guesswork. But there is a worthwhile lesson to be learnt from that little group basking on Coddem: that perhaps every seal does not act the same as every other seal. A recent study of decent monogamous house sparrows shows 10% wrong-side-of-the-blanket eggs in the nest; perhaps flipperloose and fancy free seals have 10% of dull monogamists?

Once you realise they don't all look alike, you begin to wonder if they all behave alike. That is one of the great attractions of the gentle lagoons among the reefs, where if we are quiet we can get close to the individual lives of animals and birds, and learn a little about their complexity. It would be the most wonderful compliment that could ever be paid to us – but it never has been – if, after due time, seal said to seal or eider to auntie, 'You know, once you realise they don't all look alike, you begin to wonder if they all behave alike. Perhaps these two *aren't* out to get us?'

Chapter 4

The People of the Sea

I f that thought did ever cross a sealy mind, it would not find expression in human vocables. The vocal organs of seals (as of most animals including our nearest relatives, the great apes) are not capable of producing the sounds of human speech. This should never be assumed to mean that an animal is somehow too stupid to produce the right noises: simply physically incapable of it, as we are incapable of communicating with our dogs by wagging our atrophied tails. Most dogs understand you are at least trying if you get down on all fours and waggle your bottom. Sadly, few humans try even that hard to 'talk' to other animals using the right sort of signals: we are all too ready to think that information can only be conveyed through speech, which is the favoured human signalling system. But dumb needn't necessarily mean *dumb*; the famous story of that interesting dumb human animal Helen Keller should have cured us of that error.

Seals can't talk, but they can certainly learn to respond to human speech. The grey seal Atlanta, a rescued youngster who was later returned to the wild, learned to carry out all sorts of actions on verbal signals from her trainer, H. G. Hurrell, and could also count. Her achievements are comparable to a human ten-year-old learning to detect shrimps and crabs on the seabed with her whiskers.

With *what* whiskers? Quite so. Atlanta's normal brain processes must have borne about as little relation to tests of aural comprehension and numeracy as a little girl's few pre-adolescent upper-lip hairs do to her sensory perception. A seal in a state of nature has no need of human language and no need to count. That Atlanta could understand what was required of her argues great mental flexibility and capacity for learning, as her human trainer realised. The intelligence of seals is well documented by people who have had them in their care.

So is their curiosity, which can rapidly become friendliness towards humans, once initial barriers are overcome. Most of the small fishing ports in the north of Scotland have a 'tame' seal or so, not tame enough to handle, but not wild enough to pass up the chance of free entertainment. I vividly remember a young grey seal in Oban harbour, almost close enough to touch, ignoring all the onlookers while she sniffed ecstatically towards a nearby fishing vessel, whence floated the delicious odour of frying fish. Seals underwater do not use smell to locate food; nor, for that matter, do they usually prefer it cooked: but this one had acquired new habits from her human friends.

Young, old and infirm seals must be glad enough of extra pickings, but healthy mature seals in our waters feed so well and so quickly that they can play, bask or sleep most of the day and still put on blubber. The four or five seals who haunt the fishing fleet in Stornoway are both fit and fat, and could perfectly well earn a living without titbits from the boats. I doubt if it is hunger that attracts them; more likely, once used to the noise and bustle, they enjoy watching human life go by, and find Broad Bay awfully dull by comparison.

Oddly enough, though most fishermen will curse seals and many will advocate their complete extermination, they are sheepishly tolerant of such trustful harbour scroungers. Last summer, there was an old blind bull seal near one of the reefs we sometimes visit, which is also much frequented by lobster fishermen. This poor old creature came within a few yards of our boat, and waited there confidently like a dog under a table. Every fisherman in the area breathes fire and brimstone against seals – yet somebody, if not everybody, had been throwing this one fish. It was nice to know that the human bark can be worse than the bite.

The bite is often bad enough. There is no let-up in the demand for a seal cull to 'protect' the stocks we have ravaged and the unnatural concentrations of salmon in fish farms, and there has been no assurance from the Scottish Office that it won't be met, in spite of the drastic effects of the 1988 seal sickness. So far this virus has hardly affected seals in the Hebrides; if it does, I think the seals' most implacable enemies here would pity the beasts they saw dying. This happens when there is a resurgence of myxomatosis among the local rabbits: even men who have denounced rabbits as the cause of all the crofters' woes may shake their heads and call it a horrible thing, faced with the misery of a dying rabbit unable to run away. Seeing it close to brings the horror of it home.

A dying seal at close quarters would have the same effect, or so one hopes. But where rabbits or seals, or any other creature, are not individuals – 'pets' offering trust or hapless victims dying before our eyes – they very easily become 'vermin', 'too many of them', 'too plentiful'. Systematic slaughter of indistinguishable hundreds or thousands is often easier to contemplate than the suffering or death of one recognised individual. Give them a bad collective name and hang them, gas them, trap them, shoot them – or at least hope that someone else will do it.

But even an anti-seal conversation in this part of the world is likely to end with 'Ach well, the seals were always there, and there used to be plenty fish.' There is more than a suspicion, at bottom, that the principal enemies are the huge trawlers which strain the seas empty, not the seals who have always gone about their business side by side with the modest local fishing craft. This is not surprising: anyone who works a small boat among the alien forces of water, wind and rock must feel a kind of unacknowledged reassurance from the presence of these other warm-blooded creatures, with their cowlike eyes, their doglike muzzles, their human-like hands and voices.

A reef or a seacave peopled by seals never seems threatening. The same without them might appear a place of terror, perhaps quite rightly too, to non-aquatic mammals; but they are so at home, so homely that they put you at ease. I speak as one who knows: at least once a year I pile into some fang of rock with no better reason than 'I was just looking at the seals.' They aren't deliberate sirens, just incorrigibly, beckoningly benign in their habitual contentment with life. The great naturalist Fraser Darling describes their attraction well:

His movements ashore were delightful to watch – the way he would make himself comfortable on the rock and then the expressive movements of his forelimbs, which I prefer to call hands because they can be used in ways so like the human hand, fingers and knuckles as well, rather than some awkward mittened limb of whale or manatee. You would see Old Tawny scratch his belly delicately with his fingernails, waft a fly from his nose, and then, half closing his hand, draw it down over his face and nose just as men often do. Then he would smooth his whiskers with the back of his hand, this side and that. His hands would be at rest over the expanse of his chest for a while, then you might see him scratch one palm with the fingers of the other hand, or close his fist and scratch the back of it.

It is surely this unexpected disarming humanness that lies behind the seal-into-human legends so common in the north of Scotland. In the great era of folklore collecting at the turn of the century, it was from the extreme north that these stories were taken, but they were equally prevalent in the Hebrides at an earlier date. Unfortunately, in these parts, successive religious revivals, each more dismally Presbyterian than the last, led to the suppression of 'pagan' song and folklore. To this day, even if old tales are remembered, people are often unwilling to tell them, if they smack of magic or superstition. As far as I know, the seal story only weathered it in the southern, Catholic part of the Western Isles, where in the 1920s it survived in a beautiful song collected by Marjorie Kennedy-Fraser – and doubtless embellished by her: these tireless collectors were often very creative in their efforts. The song (or 'croon': Celtic twilighters were partial to crooning) is sung by a seal, or a woman, or a seal-woman, basking on a weed-covered rock, contemplating her journey over the sea to meet her *gradhan donn* (brown-haired love). The translation is as contortedly Celtic and twilit as you would expect, but the melody is uncannily lovely – as soulful as the song of the seals themselves, which is indeed what Mrs Kennedy-Fraser believed it to be. Seals do respond to music, and I once spent half an hour rowing around the moorings at Leverburgh crooning this croon (in the twilight) to a likely looking seal. I was greatly flattered that it kept me company; but it has to be admitted that on other occasions seals have responded even more enthusiastically to Sarah's raucous renderings of *Georgie Porgie* and *Baa Baa Black Sheep*.

The seal story most widely known, at least to those ageing hippies among us who survived the Folk Boom of the sixties, is probably the ballad of the Great Silkie (or seal) of Sule Skerry. A human girl bears a child to a stranger, who disappears. As she sings to the baby, wondering about its doubtful parentage, a 'grumly guest' rises up at the foot of her bed: the Great Seal in person.

> 'I am a man upo' the land,
> I am a silkie in the sea,
> And when I'm far and far frae land,
> My home it is in Sule Skerry.'

He gives her a bag of gold to pay for the child's upbringing, until the boy is old enough to go with his seal father and learn 'tae swim his lane'. The ballad ends with stark economy, as the seal-man foresees their fate:

> 'And thou shall marry a proud gunner,
> And a proud gunner I'm sure he'll be,
> And the very first shot that e'er he shoots,
> He'll shoot both my young son and me.'

Another favourite tale concerns just such a 'proud gunner', a man who made his living from hunting seals and selling their skins for clothing and ropes. One day he crept up on a big bull seal asleep on a rock, and plunged his knife into its side, but the animal escaped to the water knife and all. That evening a knock came at the hunter's door. Outside in the windy twilight stood a great black horse with a well-dressed rider.

'If it's you that is getting sealskins, my master would do business with you,' said the stranger, when greetings were over.

'I will come tomorrow,' said the hunter, 'if you will tell me where is it he lives.'

'Ride with me now and I will take you there.'

So the hunter got up behind the horseman, and they galloped away over the fields and round the headlands, and the hunter was hanging on for dear life, with the horse pounding away at a cracking pace. At last the horse drew up, and the rider swung himself from the saddle. The hunter stared around in amazement. They stood on the edge of a cliff, with the surf booming below, and not a house or a human soul in sight.

'Where is your master's house?' he asked, beginning to be afraid.

'I will take you there,' replied the stranger, and clasping his two strong arms round the terrified hunter, he plunged with him over the cliff, down into the dark sea, darker and deeper than night. The hunter thought his end had come, but when his fright passed, he found he was moving easily through the water and, very strange it was, he was not struggling for breath. Ahead in the murk was a dim light, and as he drew near, it grew and grew, till it lit up the most wonderful sight he had ever seen. Through great gates of stone, he looked into the courtyard of a shining palace, with towers and pinnacles of coloured rock, and all made lovely with pearls and coral. Round about lay a garden of seaweed, green, brown, red and yellow, and the coloured fishes darted through that weed like sparrows in the kailyard at home. But there was sighing and sobbing in the fine gardens, and when the man looked to see who it was that wept so loud, it was not men and women that he saw, but seals. He turned then to the stranger at his side, and what did he see but another seal! Then up goes his hand to his head in fright, and what does he feel but stiff whiskers? And he was a seal himself.

'Here is my master's house,' said the seal at his side. They went through the gardens and through the halls and everywhere were seals, bowed down and sad, with the big tears rolling down their noses. And they followed after the hunter and his guide, howling so much it would break your heart to hear them. They came to a darkened room where a huge old seal lay on a bed of seaweed. In his side was a gaping wound, and by the bed lay the hunter's own knife.

'This knife,' said the guide, 'is it yours?'

When he saw how it was, that the seal he had stabbed that morning lay there dying, the hunter fell down, begging for mercy. He thought he would never see his home or his family or breathe the air again. It was in his head that the seal people had brought him there to kill him, for the hurt he had done the old seal and for the many, many others whose hides were piled in his loft at home. But at last he said, 'It is my knife, and I am sorry to say it.'

'Help us, then, and I will take you back to your home and family. Lay your hands on my father's wound and it will close.'

The hunter thought to himself, 'How can that be? I have no skill in that business.' But he did as his guide asked. And just in a minute after he had put his hands on the old seal's wound, the edges of it drew together, and his hide was like new, and up gets the old seal smoothing his whiskers, like he was just waking up. Then all the seal people were as merry as they had been sad, slapping their flippers and turning round and about, and thanking the hunter and rubbing noses with him.

Then the seal who was the son of the big old seal and the prince of all the seals said, 'There is a promise you must promise me.'

'What is that?' asked the hunter.

'Never again must you hunt seals.'

'I promise that gladly,' said the hunter.

'If you break your promise you will die, but if you keep it you will never want for fish, not at the lines or at the nets, and we will see to that.'

And the hunter swore he would keep his promise. Then he followed the prince of the seals out of the palace and out at the gates, and across the dark sea, and up through the air, and off they went on the great black horse, pounding away at a cracking pace, till they reached the man's own door, and it was still evening, with just a few stars showing in the sky. The man got down, and the prince of the seals handed him a small bag, and it was small but it was heavy.

'Long life and happiness to you, and remember your promise,' said his guide, and horse and rider galloped off into the windy twilight, before the man could say fare you well or thank you. When he went in to his house, he told his wife all the story, and she would have thought that he had gone daft, only the bag was full of gold, enough to make her a fine lady in the neighbourhood. And when she had spent it all, that was not the finish of it. The fisherman set his lines and his nets, and he never wanted for fish to eat or to sell till the end of his days. The seals were seeing to that.

A less happy tale is the legend of the seal wife. There was once a young fisherman living by himself in a hut on the seashore. His mother had died and he was too poor to get himself a wife. Life was hard for him, with no-one at home to bait his lines or cook his dinner. He had not even a whole pair of stockings to go inside his boots on Sunday, with no woman at home to knit or mend for him.

One evening, late and weary, he was sorting out his nets for the morning, and listening to the seals singing, when suddenly he forgot all about his gear. One was singing very near. And then he thought it was, not a seal singing, but a woman. So it was: there on the rocks at the edge of the sea sat a lovely girl, covered with nothing but her own brown hair, and she was combing that through with her fingers and singing all the time. The fisherman stared with his mouth open, too surprised to speak. Then he noticed that on the rock at the girl's side there was lying a spotted sealskin. Well, he made what he could of it, and a plan came into his head. He crept quiet as he could along the shore and down behind the girl, and snatched away the sealskin. She jumped up in fright, and when she saw the lad behind her, she was out of her mind, crying and pleading with him to give her back her skin.

"What does a bonny lass like you want that old skin for?' asked the fisherman, though he guessed well enough: but he spoke as nice as he could to win her to him.

'Give me my skin, please give me my skin!' cried the poor seal-woman.

'No, but I'll give you finer clothes than that. Wait you and see!'

And he ran as fast as he could back to the hut, and turned everything upside down till he got out his dead mother's dress that she was wedded in, and her Sunday shawl and shoes with silver buckles, and fine glass earrings that his father had brought from the other side of the world when he came home from the sea to marry. And he took all these fine things and a few more too down to the rocks where the poor seal-girl crouched weeping and crying 'Give me back my skin!' But he had hidden the skin already in the shed where he kept his gear. He laid all the pretty things down by her, and went back to his nets, and he had little thought of mending them, for watching what she would do. It was just as he was planning it: after a while she stopped crying, and felt the fringe of the shawl, and held the earrings up to the light, and soon there she stood all dressed up and smiling, and the fisherman had never seen anything so bonny. And now she let him tell her so and take her hand, and then he got an arm round her waist, and next a kiss, and before darkness came, she had said she would be his wife, and live with him in his hut.

54

For many years they lived in great harmony. Sons were born, and the family prospered well, for the wife did everything a wife should do about the house, and besides that she would often go to the fishing herself, and then there would be twice as big a catch as usual, which was not surprising, as she was a seal. But as time went on, the fisherman grew so used to her he was forgetting, near enough, what she was and how she had come to him, and how he had been a poor ragged lad that all the girls despised till she had made him prosper. He got a fine opinion of himself and began to neglect his wife, and she grew sad and wistful, especially when the tide was high and the surf roared; but he was not noticing that, for thinking about his grand new boat and the gold money under his mattress. Then one day when he was at sea with the boys, she thought she would tidy the shed, for she was always neat and clean. And there it was she found her own spotted sealskin, all dried up and dusty. When she saw that, she forgot about the cow needing milked and the bracken needing cut. She forgot her husband and sons and that she had ever been a human wife, and remembered only the sea caves and her seal sisters singing on the rocks. When the fisherman came home, the fire was out and the cow was mooing, and the shed was all upside down. He knew what had happened then, and remembered what she was and how she had come to him. And though he called and called her all along the shore, she never came again.

Wonderful stories, wonderful, magical seals, gentle, courteous, beautiful creatures, whose mild sad eyes are prescient of human persecution and incapable of revenge. So they are in the legends and so they are to this day. But it's still the bullet between the eyes.

Chapter 5

A Monster of the Deep

We know one hotel proprietrix who shocked us deeply by exclaiming, 'Oh goody, the 'phone! I simply *love* it when the 'phone rings, don't you?'

We could scarcely have been more nonplussed if she had asked us if we loved flagellation or cleaning lavatories. Telephones mean business – bookings – no excuse for bankruptcy – drudgery – imprisonment. We simply *hate* it when the 'phone rings. We glare at each other.

'Are you going to take it, then?'

'No, *you* take it.'

'I took it last time.' (Lie)

'I've taken at least twenty calls today.' (Gross exaggeration)

'You always say I make a mess of bookings anyway. You'd better take it.'

'It might not be a guest. It might be your mother.'

'It might be *your* mother.'

Silence.

'It's stopped.'

'Good!'

Last year we spent enormous amounts of money on room telephones, which we hoped would keep guests happy, as well as encouraging them to add substantial amounts to their bills. The system has not been a success. It turns out that some people are offended by room 'phones, which they claim destroy the impression of bucolic peace. (Peace!) Others are too mean and wily to use them, and make their calls from the kiosk at the post office instead. But many more, while they would like to make calls from their rooms, and would pay willingly for the pleasure, have found that they don't have the option: basically the system doesn't work. There are all sorts of reasons why not. The most amusing was the crow who had started to build a nest of barbed wire in our electricity transformer. This rendered the earth of our whole electrical system live. We weren't aware of the problem till Andrew got a nasty shock when attempting to sweep the chimney of the Aga. By that time it was too late: the sensitive, sophisticated electronics which control the switchboard had been zapped. But once we were earthed again and the black humming boxes had been allegedly replaced, we had a power cut. During power cuts, we found, dialled units were not charged to the appropriate extension, so that any guest could chat with his granny in Hong Kong at length and with impunity. When the power came on, every button on the switchboard flashed in scarlet distress.

'We haven't had a power cut here for ten years,' they said in Inverness.

'We get them every week!' we snarled.

The switchboard doesn't like the answering machine, either; and when earwigs run riot among the cables outside, we get poltergeists. Since power cuts, answering machine and earwigs are always with us, the telephones seldom work according to plan. However, the new system has one saving aspect: all calls in the off-season can now be diverted to Lena's house up at the back for her to deal with. I don't think she simply loves it when the 'phone rings either.

I instance the telephone only as a measure of our unusual attitude to business. We long ago decided that it was better to have free time than money, and these days calculate the amount of business we take very finely, so that we can just stay personally solvent and can offer our staff the same level of work and wages as usual – but no more. Accordingly, we all work a fortnightly rota for the twenty-four week season, with the place open for eleven days and closed for three, and we also close for a week during the school holidays. This keeps everyone tolerably sane. Fixing days off is the first bit of forward planning we do every winter, before taking any bookings for the next season; and we have all learned by experience not to let anyone (however well-behaved, well-lined or well-connected) wheedle in on those sacrosanct days off.

But of course, there's nothing we can do to warn casual comers of this brutal regime. So on weekends off they still turn up: in the rain, on foot, ninety years old today, on honeymoon, having driven from London, sailed from Dublin, flown from New York just to knock on our door. The inns are full, the cafés are shut, the island Sabbath is at hand, wherein no man can obtain food, drink or petrol. Their stories are heartrending, our guilt crushing. But we don't relent: no! We leave explanations to Lena, and bolt.

Nine times out of ten, bolting is done in the rain, and consists in cowering in the office with the door locked and heads below sill level, or sitting in the car in a passing place till the coast is clear. But in early summer, when the weather is at its best and we are not yet the gibbering wrecks we later become, we sometimes plan our escape ahead, and organise family camping expeditions. When Sarah was about four, we decided we really ought to camp, when possible, to encourage her to be self-reliant and to keep a stiff upper lip when faced with burnt fried eggs, sour milk, wet sleeping bags and lumpy ground. It must be said that after four years of this character-building exercise, she has learnt not only to be stoical about charcoal in the soup and midges everywhere, but actually to like camping.

We have one with us who sticketh closer than any brother. He likes camping too – he camps with enormous, even appalling enthusiasm; but he has not learnt to be stoical about anything. I speak, of course, of Jet, alias the Monster.

His disposition is optimistic. Camping is such fun – but it could be made even better, if only people would organise things properly ahead, with due attention to certain important points. These sleeping bags, for a start: much too tight! It's not at all companionable for everyone to be zipped into an individual cocoon, and there really isn't room to snuggle down in one with a human friend. All that happens is the zip bursts and lets in horrid cold draughts. Then the only warm place to lie is on Sarah's head, but she squirms about and is rather scrawny and knobbly anyway. A mattress and a couple of downies would improve things next time. And the tent's a bit small: the humans probably don't intend to kick, but they never seem to learn that when a tired Labrador rests his head on a pair of ankles, it's very upsetting when his pillow twitches from under him. Growling doesn't seem to cure them of fidgeting, either. A few nice soft pillows to go with the mattress and downies would be a good thing. Then there's the problem of entrances and exits. It's bad enough having to operate the tent zip with your own rather valuable and sensitive nose, in spite of repeatedly asking those with hands to do it for you: but then to be shouted at for standing in the eggs – in the dark! How could one know? – and for letting the rain in, and for coming back with wet feet, that's really more than any dog should have to put up with. *Someone* has to go out to check all's well. It's *terra incognita* out there. There might be wolves – lions – dog-eating sharks – isn't that sea nearer than it was when we went to bed? Shouldn't they get up and look? Aren't they *worried* about dog-eating sharks? Perhaps they're just too stupid to realise the dangers. Anyway it must be breakfast time – takes them a while to get the fire going, specially in the rain. That's another thing that could be improved on: the sausages were burnt, and covered in sand too. Better remind them how I like mine done. And what's this I see? A whole loaf of bread, all nicely sliced and buttered. How thoughtful! That just fills a gap till they've got something more substantial ready for me. Camping's such fun!

Sometimes some of us feel camping would be more fun if it weren't for Monster. When we first got an enthusiasm for it, we kitted ourselves out with rucksacks, so that we could backpack to remote spots, perhaps for a few nights consecutively, with hikes in between. But Monster's Improved Camping Régime soon made this unlikely. *He* couldn't be asked to carry a rucksack, and there simply wasn't room to pack into ours the items he finds necessary for even one night's camp, let alone more: feeding bowl, drinking bowl, meat, dog-meal, rawhide chews, three towels, a woolly rug, a downie, collar and lead, and a large bottle of water just in case a sudden drought falls on the land. This last is really a piece of lunacy, but I always lose my nerve and include it at the last minute. He would be so offended if there were nothing to drink but Perrier and Pepsi Cola; the bubbles make him sneeze. In any event, the rest of his luggage is so bulky that really we need to take the car, and camp near it. In fact, he finds the car necessary to retire to for a comfortable nap while the rest of us set up the tent in the rain or wash up burnt greasy pans in cold salt water.

When we first bought *Sand Eel*, we looked forward to slightly more adventurous camping. The boat holds as much gear as the car, so Jet would not have to lack for necessaries, yet it's much more exciting camping on uninhabited islands than by roadside ditches. We were a little apprehensive about what his reaction would be when he discovered no car convenient to his campsite. Where would he shelter from the rain? How would he stand Sarah's incessant babbling for a whole evening, when it is his usual habit to meditate quietly in the car between five o'clock and bedtime? But our first family camping experience had been carless, by rubber dinghy across the Northton shallows, and he hadn't been too disconcerted. He had had to have my jumper and jacket draped over him to keep out the keen evening air, and had splashed vigorously out of and into the inflatable all the way home, but *he* hadn't seemed to suffer from the cold or damp. So for our first camping trip in *Sand Eel*, we took him to Ensay, which is his favourite island, to give him a good impression of the new hobby. After the usual traumatic voyage, we landed and put up the tent, with Monster helping, and had a picnic lunch. After that, an awful problem presented itself. Jet's day is divided between walks, meals and naps in the car. When none of these is happening, he squeaks and howls against the unfeeling cruelty of those who would deprive him of his rights. We had left the car on Leverburgh pier and there was no meal planned for at least another five hours. We bore half an hour of increasingly pitiful howling and then began to walk. We walked all round the island and along the top as well, quite slowly, to spin it out. We would have gone more slowly still, if we hadn't attracted the attention of the resident bull. Bulls always seem to dislike Jet. Jet, on the other hand, shows great determination in getting as near any bull as possible, in order to swagger under his nose and waddle between him and his cows. In spite of our vigilance, he contrived to sidle off and do just this to the Ensay bull, who until he saw Jet had been placidly scratching his bottom on a gatepost. We seized Monster and hustled him out of sight, but the bull's equanimity was ruffled. He sniffed the air, shifted uneasily from foot to foot, and exclaimed to himself in the fractious squealing undertone of a bull whose day has been spoiled. For the next mile I whipped everyone along at a spanking pace. Andrew jeered, Sarah grumbled, and Jet dawdled: but every time I looked back I saw the bull purposefully plodding after us, till rising ground hid him from sight. We arrived back at the tent rather earlier than planned. Monster ate a monstrous dinner, and immediately gave way to loud expressions of woe because no car was available for his post-prandial nap. I made Sarah's tea and he interrupted his plaints to eat most of that as well. Eating her food is one thing, but sharing her lair is another, definitely infra dig: so when she went to bed, he remained outside the tent, exhausted, fretful, and vociferous. Where was his car, his bed, his sofa? He stared across the Sound towards home, filmy-eyed, and began to shiver. We had planned a modest treat for ourselves, with lentil curry to heat up and cans of lager; but under Monster's alternately baleful and despairing gaze, the food stuck in our throats. He doesn't like lentils, or lager. 'I wish we'd brought a few T-bone steaks,' said Andrew. Jet agreed, wincing, that this would have made things much better. Might he suggest that next time . . . ?

We returned from that camping trip not relaxed or refreshed, and too frayed in nerves, really, to appreciate the excellent opportunities to cultivate stiff upper lip afforded by Monster. Our enthusiasm for camping voyages waned. The occasional boating picnic was as much as we could bear: at least after one of these shorter forays on the deep, we could count on Monster sleeping off the day in the car afterwards, allowing us a peaceful evening to recover from his seadoggery. The next time we stayed on Ensay, we begged a loan of the empty dilapidated mansion house there. Jet found this more worth the horrors of a sea voyage than sleeping under canvas. There was a sofa, rather damp, but passable, and a semiferal cat to torment. The imposing flight of steps leading down to the beach was a dignified stance for an old Admiral, from which he could survey the whole northern part of the Sound, musing on past conquests and triumphs: the saving of the Flagship off Killegray, the routing of twenty stout rams on Saghay, the appropriation of a whole packet of Penguin biscuits between Suem and Sleicham. He bore up heroically to the absence of his car, howling only intermittently.

If you live on an island as remote as Harris, the only holiday you can have without prolonged and expensive travelling is on a neighbouring island. We had decided we would spend our week off in July on North Uist. For Andrew and me, the main attraction was the chance of sailing across in *Sand Eel*, and of exploring some of the tortuous channels and unknown islands on the south side of the Sound, where we had never been before. We had a great desire to negotiate Rangas, the mile-long reef split for its whole length by a channel only fifteen feet wide in places; to moor in the

Opsay Basin, a calm lagoon circled through 330° of land, set in the dangerous wilderness of rock and water like one of Brendan's legendary havens; to walk on the machair of Boreray, reputedly the most beautiful of all the jewels of the Sound, with its shifting white sands and tranquil freshwater loch full of wildfowl. We pored over charts and maps, as agog with our little adventure as more seasoned travellers might be before portaging up the Orinoco. We had booked a cottage for the week and Lena, whose husband had no holiday at that time, had agreed to come with us. She would take Sarah and her own children over on the little foot-ferry, and entertain them with beaches and picnics, while we sailed in blissful childless silence, a whole day at a time. The overfalls of Berneray – the shifting sandbanks of Lingay – the Yellow Rocks of Splears – the Grey Horse Channel: all this and more! Chimborazo and Cotopaxi could never charm as these names could, with the West Coast of Scotland Pilot's gloomy presentiments and the uncharted area south and west of Berneray to get the adrenalin flowing.

But we had forgotten someone. Like the bad fairy at Thorn Rose's christening, Monster lurked blackly in the wings, with evil intent. It is his policy never to let both of us out of his sight at once, unless he is resting in his car; furthermore, he carves up babysitters on principle. He might just about tolerate Lena: he is very fond of her, as she did him many services in the days before he came to us – rescuing him from a dustbin, for example; but there is no need to dwell here on those humiliating events of puppyhood. But then bearing in mind his present arthritic condition, how was Lena going to cope with the conflicting demands of one stiff and stately Labrador, and three lively children? Monster will not be hurried, and when he has waddled as far as he thinks fit, all seventy pounds of him lies down with monumental finality. If abandoned, he immediately sets up a loud and far-carrying wail which attracts sympathetic onlookers from miles around. If Lena rushed off to rescue children from clifftops or whirlpools, she wouldn't have gone a hundred yards before someone had telephoned the SSPCA. We would return from our sail to find the children drowned and Monster taken into care.

The only way to save our sailing plans was to take the car: then Jet would sleep peacefully in it in his accustomed manner from after breakfast till half past two; the children could work off their energy in the morning, so that they would be docile enough by afternoon to accompany him on his leisurely constitutional without disappearing into the nearest quicksand. He would then dine and retire again to his car to digest, and we would guarantee to be home for his evening entertainment. Lena good-naturedly agreed to all this. The only problem was *how* to get the car to North Uist. The Harris–Uist foot-ferry takes people, bicycles, dogs, sacks of mussels, and the groceries for Berneray, but not motor vehicles. The car ferry leaves from and arrives at different ports, travels direct only two days a week, and costs an extra £50. But there was nothing else for it; in the end Andrew had to spend the appropriate day in the week preceding our holiday delivering the car to a convenient point in Monster's projected progress. Like the aristocracy of old, he sends his servants ahead to prepare for his coming: we call it making straight the way of the Lord.

Our plans were not perfect even yet. The Lord himself still had to be conveyed. The wings of the cherubim might have done the trick, but we really could not expect Lena to hoist seventy pounds of struggling Labrador from the slippery pier into the bobbing *Endeavour*, suffer an hour of his loud protests and attempts to abandon ship, and disembark him on the equally slippery pier at Newton. She offered, and the three children claimed they would help, but it was unthinkable: someone would drown, and it wouldn't be Monster.

He would have to sail instead with us in *Sand Eel*, a six-hour voyage.

'It isn't worth it!' I cried in despair, almost cracking when I realised the horror of the situation. 'Let's just leave the boat behind. We'll take him on the ferry.'

Andrew was determined. 'You take him on the ferry if you like. I'm sailing.'

That settled it. I certainly wasn't going to have *him* drown in these unknown waters, leaving me as sole guardian of Monster's declining years.

So began Monster's most epic voyage. For the first half hour, he swaggered in his smart blue and white doggy lifejacket, scenting the breeze and squaring his shoulders. But when he saw Ensay fall astern, he sank down whimpering in the bilges; and when *Sand Eel* hit the wallowing swell west of Killegray, he wedged himself between a sailbag and the centreplate case, and lay mute and frozen with tight shut eyes for the rest of the voyage.

Never has dog been so glad to see car. In fact, he attached himself so firmly to it that it was difficult to winkle him out of it for the rest of the holiday. He lay as if glued to the back seat, nose pressed to one end and tail to the other, clinging on with all four paws. The children had to travel everywhere illegally in the boot. They were glad of the car too: it opened up the possibilities of ice cream shops. Two Funny Feet, one Fat Frog, and one Hazelnut Cornetto, please. Can you guess who the Cornetto is for?

Chapter 6

Behold a Pale Horse

'Do you know,' said Andrew at breakfast time, 'they've managed to isolate DNA from mammoths in Russia? They might be able to produce a mammoth from an elephant.'

'Make an elephant into a mammoth?' asked Sarah through the Weetabix.

'No, but make it have a mammoth baby.'

Theoretically, we are Against Genetic Engineering, but the prospect of live mammoths is a strong temptation to apostasy.

'There used to be mammoths in Britain,' contributed Sarah, with blatant visions of a new pet.

'And beavers,' said Andrew, wistfully.

'And woolly rhinoceroses,' I mused.

'And wild horses,' Andrew went on.

We all considered Britain's more glorious past.

'Come to think of it,' Andrew added rather gloomily, 'there still *are* wild horses.'

He was referring, of course, to Erica. The name *Erica*, as Sarah frequently expounds it, is the feminine form for Eric, meaning kingly, and Erica is therefore queenly. In fact, the brute has the mental makeup more traditionally attributed to the peasant – self-interested cunning, extreme suspicion and inveterate laziness. She will usually move if someone runs in front of her with a handful of pony-nuts, but when the pony-nuts are finished she will kick the bearer, buck off her rider and head for home. Every month that passes convinces me more thoroughly that Erica was one of the worst mistakes of our domestic lives. But I am alone in my disapprobation; over Andrew and Sarah she continues to queen it.

Erica is of the Eriskay strain. Enthusiasts describe the breed as beautiful, intelligent, docile, affectionate, wonderfully hardy, economical to feed; the ancient horses whose features appear on Pictish carvings, the heroic steeds of Cuchulain. Detractors laugh at their short legs and enormous heads, and claim they are not a separate breed at all, but simply workaday nags which have degenerated in size because of dismal conditions on the island where they run wild. So far, they have been denied formal Rare Breeds status, so perhaps the detractors are winning.

During the eighteenth and nineteenth centuries, local strains of semi-wild Scottish hill pony were improved with cob and Clydesdale blood to make them more suitable for heavy draught work. The result was something like the modern Highland Pony, large and heavily built, stronger than its antecedents, but with a larger appetite: such ponies could not fend for themselves in winter – not that any pony should have to. Whether the modern Eriskay survived untouched by such improvement of stock because Eriskay was a very small and unimportant island, or whether the ponies there reverted rapidly to type because of poor feeding, will probably remain a moot point. All that is known for sure is that in the herd running semi-wild there in the 1950s, only mares were left, until an exported gelding sent to Barra was found not to have had the op after all. This Eric was fetched back forthwith and a breeding programme enthusiastically instituted by a local vet. To achieve sufficient genetic variation, Highland mares of similar appearance and size (under thirteen and a half hands) were used, so that an Eriskay pony can be grade A, B or C. Erica is grade B. She has a grade A friend along the road who is a hand shorter, just as pretty and just as wilful.

Whatever the truth about Eriskay ancestry (true lyricists claim an Arabian forefather swam ashore from a wrecked galleon of the Armada) it has to be admitted that to a layman's eye, all indigenous northern strains of everything are far more like each other than like anything else: squat, hairy, hardy, resourceful, wily as water and stubborn as rock, whether ponies, sheep, goats or humans, from the Welsh mountains, the Cumbrian fells, or the bleak islands of the North and West. Erica is without doubt superbly adapted to her environment: to torrents of rain cascading off her thick grey coat, to turning broad quarters to the gale, to digging potatoes with her small neat feet, to unfastening latches with her clever nose; but not to doing as she is told.

We bought her (indeed, begged her previous owner to part with her) after drinking rather too much of a rather nice claret one summer evening. Sarah had always wanted a pony, and had just been sent some money by her grandfather. Under the influence of whatever beguiling château it was, it seemed like a wonderful idea to surprise her by spending the cash on her behalf; and by Sarah, this particular wonderful idea was judged a great success. Erica can do no wrong, not by bucking, kicking, rolling on her rider or bolting.

Erica, for a time, had been enrolled at a riding school as a mount for the disabled. It was soon my firm conviction that she had been expelled from school for disabling those who were mounted on her. Certainly, by the time we met her, after a six months' sabbatical, she had decided equitation was a mug's game; and the cunning brain inside her capacious skull soon worked out who the mugs were. We are not a horsy family, but we had hopefully divided our field into two smart paddocks for Erica (the rails, in a timberless land, costing three times as much as the pony) and we had bought a book. We waited till Sarah was out of the way so that there should be no distractions for Erica's first trial. Andrew went out with the bridle over his arm, the book (open at diagram) in his hand, and carrots in his pockets.

'For God's sake keep that bridle out of sight!' I implored. I had a sort of feeling.

Erica looked mild and grey, and nuzzled affectionately into his pocket.

'Don't be silly. She's lovely and friendly, aren't you, old girl?'

Erica munched carrots agreeably, but there was a gleam in her eye.

'Can't you hide that book?' I asked, nervously.

'No, I need to look at it.'

Erica looked at it too, sardonically.

'The book says always tie them up before you do anything else,' Andrew explained. He clipped the lead rope into Erica's head collar, hitched it to one of the nice new fenceposts, and approached her with bit and bridle held as in the diagram. Erica reared up at once, pulling five yards of fence with her and breaking her head collar.

We had a spare collar. Andrew got it on her with some difficulty. I stood well back and said she was a horrible brute. She flourished her heels.

'She's not a horrible brute! It's my fault, I should have tied her to something stronger – the gatepost. She won't get that out of the ground in a hurry.'

Having found she couldn't get it out of the ground at all, Erica plunged and reared like a rodeo colt, grazed her chest on the fence, and with a final frenzied effort broke the new collar and careered off down the field. It took the better part of a week to persuade her to stand still longer than was necessary to gobble our offerings of carrots and apples. Then suddenly she became meek. She permitted a head collar and a saddle, and let herself be led round for a few days with children on her back. She graduated to bridle and bit, with protest, but of the sort which expressed the pain and terror of a noble soul, rather than mulish obstinacy.

'She can't have been used to the bit,' we decided. 'They must have just led her with the head collar, for disabled riders.' (It was much later that we found she had been used to taking the bit three or four times a day, though only with sufficient Polo mints to make it worth her while.) We comforted her with apples, and found she could eat them quite well even with the bit in. So virtuous did she now seem that Andrew decided it was mean to leave her head collar on permanently. For several days in succession, she stood with saintly patience, untethered, while he bridled her. Then one day he put the saddle on first. Erica kicked up her heels, bucked, skipped and capered round her paddock, unbridled, unhaltered and uncatchable. We capered after her, scattering carrots and pony-nuts, cajoling, swearing, and soon panting too much to do either. For such a slow fat middle-aged pony, Erica proved surprisingly nimble, with a nifty way of presenting her heels where you thought her forelock ought to be. After an hour, we gave up and telephoned her previous owner. He sounded reassuring, and said she must learn who was boss: she might need a touch of the stick. He came along to help, stick in hand, and attempted a touch of it on her bottom, only to find the same surprising prevalence of heels as we had. We all leant on the paddock rail and stared at her in dismay. She shook her mane and jeered, then lay down and rolled defiantly on her saddle.

Unable to stand the humiliation any longer, we went out for the afternoon. When we returned, Erica stood forlorn, without an audience. Her head drooped, and the saddle had slipped under her tummy. When we went up to her, she reared and kicked as a matter of form, but her eyes showed she was secretly glad to see us. Only human hands could remove that horrid saddle.

Since then, she has been quite friendly, but it can hardly be claimed (though Andrew and Sarah do claim it frequently) that she is a good girl. She hustles ladies with handbags, digs up the potato patch, raids the dustbins and holds the fruit and vegetable van up to ransom. She doesn't mind being ridden, but the decision as to direction and pace must rest with her. Quite often, she prefers simply to stand still; but at other times she likes to career up and down sand dunes in equine frolic.

Sarah had a lesson on a civilised pony while we were on holiday. 'He walked on when I asked him, and when the lady just clicked her tongue, he trotted!' she exclaimed in wonder. 'And I asked what we should do about Erica to make her good. She said we should just relax.'

Erica hardly needs that advice. She spends more time than any horse I have ever seen lying down, even with a rider on her back.

There is one thing Erica is very obliging about: she keeps the grass down in our field. We used to assume, in our ignorance, that by debarring sheep, we were encouraging a rich growth of wild flowers, with attendant birds, bees and butterflies. So we were, for the first two years; larks and corncrakes nested in the long grass, and the drier areas sported all the lovely machair flowers, wild pansy, poppy, alkanet, purple and yellow vetches. But then growth deteriorated. The annual flowers were strangled by moss and dead grass, till insidious ragwort and knapweed were almost all that was left. We cut hay for a few seasons, but haymaking in Harris rain and midges (always one or the other and sometimes both) is not the bucolic joy it looks in Brueghel's version, and anyway as we had at that time no herbivorous animals of our own, we had to beg people to come and take it away after all the labour of making it. Reluctantly, we decided we must have it grazed – reluctantly, because of the few struggling shrubs we had managed to nurture: sheep and cows which are kept on grassland are always ravenous for hard forage, and much prefer shrubs to grass. Any beasts put to graze would have to be tethered. Lena's husband Uisdeann supplied a series of tetherable beasts, rams and cows. They did their best, though the circular mow of an animal on a tether never looks tidy, and were picturesque, especially the cows – 'lawn mooers', in the children's parlance. The most imposing was the Simmenthal. Uisdeann had bought her in a rash moment, not calculating what a vast amount of fodder such a large animal would need: crossbred local cows are much smaller. She was delighted with her summer grass, and became exceedingly popular with guests. Unwittingly, she sorted them immediately into three categories. The nervous were asking 'Is that a bull?' almost before they got out of their cars, and the positively paranoid didn't believe 'no' even when we pointed to her rear end and allowed her to lick our faces in a demonstration of amiability. The sunny optimists exclaimed at dinner 'Oh, how lovely, cream from your own cow!' and looked offended when it was pointed out that she was a beef breed, and would indeed become beef if she didn't manage a calf pretty quick. The shy and solitary made a confidante of her, and could be seen pouring out their troubles into her friendly ears. I never dared ask what became of her, but I know she didn't look set to produce a calf.

Moonlight was another bovine visitor. She was short and tubby, black except for the comical white face which gave her her name, but she had sex appeal. When she was with us, we had daily visits from the local bull. He simply stomped through the cattle grid, placing his feet carefully between the bars; but he couldn't be driven out that way, in case in agitation he broke a leg. In fact, he never looked agitated at all, being an extremely laid-back animal, but to be on the safe side he had to be got out through the small gate, a very tight squeeze. Uisdeann had to push him hard from behind to get him through, which we would certainly not have ventured ourselves even with such a mild bull as that one; but Uisdeann, like many men who work with large animals, treats bulls as children do pussycats.

Uisdeann's rams, though handsome and horny, were not as soothing company as the cows. Whoever moved the iron peg to which they were tethered had to watch out for an unexpected butt in the backside, and on the whole they were not responsive to conversation or caresses. But though adult sheep lack rapport with humans, it is a different matter with their offspring. Lambs are so easily subverted to human ways that they will live in your house if you let them. The inevitable bottle-fed orphans are a highlight of the children's year, and it has to be admitted that the adults enjoy them too. They don't do anything as useful as grazing the field: they switch with delinquent suddenness from milky innocence to garden rape, at which stage they are bundled off to join the rest of the flock. But before they get their taste for herbaceous plants, they are much-indulged pets, noisy, demanding and playful. They are usually bursting in and out of Lena's kitchen or ours, bleating loudly for their bottles. A lamb's bleat is very piercing indoors, and if uttered when the hatch to the dining room is open, it causes great amusement on the other side. The only way to suppress them other than by feeding them is to run them to exhaustion, and if there are no children at home to occupy them, Lena can often be seen frisking and gambolling up and down the drive with a pair of lusty lambs at her heels, in the hope of half an hour's peace later. How the dour staid adults can produce such cheerful riotous youngsters is an annual puzzle of sheep psychology.

Handreared lambs are of course completely unafraid of the dogs with whom they share a kitchen or fireside. Jet regards them affectionately, nuzzling and licking them with just a hint of Big Bad Wolf in his rolling eye and drooling chops: but their familiarity is embarrassing for a self-respecting collie, and after a week or so of sulks, Uisdeann's Shep chooses to ignore them loftily. This is not always easy: one year's orphans admired him so much that they followed him everywhere. Shep has an irrepressible habit of chasing cars, and Snowy and Star soon learned to do likewise. Unlike their hero, though, they did not have sufficient delicacy to distinguish between the vehicles of customers and those of postmen and other no 'count persons. Guests were astonished to find themselves hounded down the drive by the two woolly bandits, and our explanation that they thought they were sheepdogs did not really make things much clearer.

When not chasing cars, lambs are guaranteed guest-softeners. Lena usually has a waiting-list of ladies desperate for a turn at bottle-feeding the little darlings.

But since Erica came, we have no grass to spare for lawn-mooers or lawn-meehers. In fact, there may soon be no grass for Erica

either. Rabbits have moved in. The only two humane discourage-
ments to rabbits that I have heard of are leopard pee and long wet
grass. We have no access to an obliging leopard, but we used to
have long grass, and it was usually wet. Since Erica grazed it down,
the rabbits have poured in to crop every new blade that pushes
through the soil. We try to ignore their burrows in the field, but
embarrassingly they have started on the front lawn. The only
solution would seem to be an SOS to Edinburgh Zoo.

Chapter 7

Happy Families

The cliff-bound bay of Liuri is an awesome place. However you approach it, from the wilderness coastline beyond Rubh' an Teampuill, or from the clifftops and blowholes of Toe Head, it comes in sight suddenly, a great black concavity in the 400-foot precipice where the long ridge of Chaipaval drops off into the sea. It is impossible to stand back far enough to make it small, or to get near enough to make it familiar. Scrambling to right or left throws up further folds of hillside, further wedges of impassable cliffs sheer to the water's edge. One is forced upwards to the rounded brow of Chaipaval, and Liuri disappears without ever becoming tangible. There is nothing to be done with it, no means of approach, no way of assimilating it to the class of Places-I-have-been. It remains as tantalisingly distant as scenery in a painting.

And what a painting: what frowning pinnacles, what wallowing surf, what sombre gloom slashed with what ecstatic rays of light! But no, the subject would not have suited, in the days when dedicated interpreters of landscape roamed remote parts in search of the Gothic or the Sublime. It was Keats, I think, who complained against the Scottish (or more likely, *Scotch*) landscape for being unclassical. The same feeling was expressed in less elevated terms by some friends of ours who said the Hebrides were 'just like the Greek islands, but without the temples in the foreground.' The foreground lacks temples; the heights lack castles; the whole lacks human figures, or even picturesque reminders of the noble ambition, the spiritual aspiration, the horrid fate of any human being past or present. It totally lacks human interest: it is not interested in humans in the least, it gets by quite well without them. The nineteenth century wouldn't have stood for it. I can imagine the aquatint, with a plaid-clad Highlander peering over the cliff; the etching, with the captain's fair daughter clinging to the wrecked spars in the surf; the Academy canvas, with a plump Andromeda rolling her eyes among the shattered blocks at the water's edge. But Liuri is more austere art, broken perpendiculars, vaulting light, luminous shadow, vibrantly ticked with white and flaked with green.

The last description is as affected, as distorted as any of the former. Nature is not art; the attempt to get close to it by making it an aesthetic experience is a falsification. The Highlander and the Andromeda are not there, but the aesthetic sense, beavering away to pull it into line with its own conception of fittingness, insists that they should be: only thus will the place acquire human meaning. A century or so later, when fashions in seeing have changed (and what is fashionable is always thought fitting) I can see, not a flabby pink and gold girl where there is no human life, but an abstract arrangement of texture and colour where there are living things, white ticks for warm, breathing, breeding fulmars, green flakes for growing tufts of campion and roseroot. I don't know which is the greater sin. That isn't the way to get into Liuri, where a thousand fulmars glide and brood and a thousand shags crane below them.

Fulmar: of which Martin Martin says 'It is a grey Fowl about the size of a Moorhen. It has a strong Bill with wide Nostrils . . . When anyone approaches the *Fulmar* it spits out at its Bill about a Quart of pure Oil; the Natives surprise the Fowl, and preserve the Oil, and burn it in their Lamps: it is good against *Rheumatick* Pains and Aches in the Bones . . . some take it for a Vomit, others for a Purge. It has been successfully us'd against *Rheumatick* Pains in Edinburgh and London.'

Shag: F. S. Beveridge commends the bird thus: 'Held in great esteem by the natives, who make soup out of it . . . if properly made it is very like the best hare soup.'

I have never tried fulmar oil for my aching bones, but I have cooked shag, and though it did indeed taste like the very best hare, I have come to believe that the secrets of places like Liuri will not be revealed to the seeker after cures for Rheumaticks or hare soup: the camel is not more constrained in the eye of the needle.

That is perhaps unfair, or at least unfair to the past. The hard-pressed inhabitants of St Kilda, who could not have lived at all if they had not lived on seabirds (but who might have lived longer if their midwives hadn't persisted in anointing the umbilical cord with rancid fulmar oil) were both knowledgeable about the habits of the birds they hunted and passionately attached to their wild island home. The same must be true of any people who subsist primarily on a natural food source, and who can only exist at all by virtue of their own skill and daring in pursuit of it. It depends where you are, of course: it doesn't require much skill or daring to unzip a bunch of bananas when they fall in your lap, but it's different catching fulmars with bare hands on a sheer precipice a thousand feet high. As long as there is a real risk of famine or accident attendant on hunting animals – or even bananas – as prey, the attitude of the hunter can never be simply utilitarian. Success in such hunting requires intimate knowledge of the hunted, and accords to it proper respect and gratitude, as to the bringer of all good things. 'Can the world exhibit a more valuable commodity? . . . Deprive us of the Fulmar and St Kilda is no more,' declared an eighteenth-century St Kildan. I don't know where he picked up his Augustan turn of phrase, but I'm prepared to believe he said something at least similarly warm. This is very different from our present-day attitude to the supermarket shopping basket, except as portrayed in the television commercials. In fact it is doubtful whether such an attitude survives in the Western world at all, if it does anywhere. In a money economy, everything has its price, and the necessities of life are provided by that price, not by the catch or harvest in itself. If the price is high, the temptation to take two or three or a hundred times the sensible quota and make two or three or a hundred times the money is not even a temptation – it becomes a virtue in the family and in the community. Whether the harvest is monoculture wheat with a run off of nitrates and a destination in the EEC wheat mountain or wolfpelts gathered by motorised Innuit slung with the latest in modern artillery, it is reducible to a figure in pounds or dollars.

But what of present-day hunters, the men and women with expensive rods and guns and esoterically labelled breeches and waistcoats? They can be conveniently divided into three groups. The first (the largest) like killing – a natural enough liking, but not very valuable at this stage in our planetary history. The second like fresh fish and the best hare soup, a coarse but cheerful reason for doing things in. The third are the elite, altogether more sensitive and thinking than the other two: as they will tell you themselves, they love to be out in the wilds, at one with nature, locked in an atavistic contest of wits and strength with a respected adversary.

The cynical observer may notice, however, that they are unwilling to enter the contest without improving on nature by the addition of high-tech tackle, high velocity rifles, advanced wet-weather gear and knowledgeable ghillies. Nevertheless, this refined third class might seem to have a point: wouldn't we all like to get back to nature, weren't we all hunters in our origins, can't we recapture the primitive Eden in the excitement of the chase?

I think the answer has to be that we can't. There is no Eden without innocence, and we lost that long ago. We eradicated a great many other species in the process, from the giant herbivores of the Pleistocene to the British beaver and the American passenger pigeon, which used to darken the sky in its migratory hordes just a hundred years ago. After all that bloody past, the only paradise humans can expect to reach by killing things is a fool's paradise. The role of super-predator comes all too easily to us.

But if converse with nature is not to be on aesthetic or exploitative grounds, what conversation can there be at all? I should say that if the aesthetic approach is faith, an overwhelming belief in something that isn't there ('I wish I'd brought my camera!') and exploitation is hope ('What's in it for me?'), then you are left with charity, which suffereth long and is kind, and knows when to shut up – it is high time I shut up, and spoke more of fulmars: my point is only, that many people nowadays have the previously unimaginable privilege of being able to view wild nature with love, not as a store to be plundered or an alien force to be tamed, or even as a Prospect to be admir'd. I doubt there is anything to be ashamed of in enjoying that privilege, or anything to be valued in the attitude which sees nothing good where there is no direct benefit to humanity. That was a valuable attitude once: it could destroy us now.

But back to fulmars. It isn't difficult to love them, because they are so loving to each other. A pair of fulmars tucked side by side at the nest personify domestic harmony. They are comparatively long-lived birds, which don't breed till about their seventh year, although possibly they pair up before then. This is not unknown among birds: albatrosses may become 'engaged' a year or more before they are ready to breed. As with many other long-lived birds, they appear to be faithful to the same mates year after year, each pair frequenting their nesting ledge from February or March, two months before egg laying. A few, in fact, only desert the site for a couple of months in autumn, when they are at sea building up the fat reserves they have lost whilst rearing the young. Until a hundred years ago, their only British base was St Kilda. Now they have spread to practically every suitable cliff in Britain, and sometimes to buildings and ruins or inland sites as well. They nest colonially, but some groups are very small, just two or three pairs. Young birds may be seen prospecting a likely stretch of uncolonised coast in summer; the following spring, new nests may appear.

Why they should be expanding their range when other species are declining is not entirely clear, but it is probably to do with their unspecialised feeding habits. Like gulls, fulmars will take any sort of fish, and are also happy when trawls are hauled in, or when fish offal is discarded at sea. In other words, wasteful human habits actually benefit this bird, a very different position from, say, auks, which depend entirely on sand-eels for feeding their young. This varied feeding not only makes a fat bird, it leaves a reserve of about half a pint of oil in the stomach, the same which is potent against *Rheumatick* pains. If threatened, the bird vomits this out in a stream which fortunately smells loathsome to interfering humans.

Before I ever saw a fulmar, I had often heard of the stinking oil which these birds would spit at you, notching up direct hits, it would seem, with malevolent glee. I expected a creature at least as belligerent as a blackback. In fact, they are the least aggressive birds I have ever handled. We have had two separate beached and exhausted fulmars brought to us for rest and feeding prior to release. Neither was a successful rescue: but not only did these birds not spew oil at us, they didn't try to peck either. Their oil reserves were probably used up because of poor feeding, but both would have been quite strong enough to peck. Perhaps they were aware we meant no harm: you often read a claim to this effect in fictional or highly coloured accounts of rescuing wild creatures, but I have never seen it in real life, except possibly with these fulmars. Fulmar chicks are more likely than the adults to eject oil at intruders: a sort of choking noise and movement gives the warning. When newly hatched, they are said to be a menace to their own parents in this respect. A friend of ours once had the care of a golden eagle which in its youthful idiocy had preyed on fulmar chicks, till it became so oiled it collapsed into the sea and would have drowned if it hadn't been rescued. Once past the vulnerable flightless stage, fulmars are far less likely to spit, unless cornered and in real terror. I have never seen fulmars spitting oil in what pass for territorial disputes, or at the puffins and rabbits which sometimes share their nesting sites.

There is no more peaceful way to spend an afternoon than lying on a clifftop watching fulmars. They like reasonable shelter at their breeding sites, so you may often find a group on the sunnier side of a narrow inlet (a geo, in local parlance) where they can be watched from the opposite lip. They are not easily disturbed: birds on the nest will look back at an observer with a calm dark eye, and those flying in and out will glide unhurriedly close and curious, on stiff silent wings. They prefer to nest among vegetation, so that the most prized sites are often clustered along earthy or rubbly veins in the rock, where a mat of sea-campion or thrift or a miniature lawn of emerald green grass makes comfort for a fulmar. There is next to no nest building, but I have frequently seen a sitting fulmar rearranging the leaves round her: which is perhaps where the St Kildans got the idea that the fulmar eats sorrel. A pair of courting fulmars in their cliff garden is a lovely sight. All their movements are gentle and graceful, and they talk to each other in an affectionate undertone. Occasionally, an intruder will land on the ledge, particularly if it is one of the coveted cushions of greenery. This bird sidles forward bashfully, with head turned aside to persuade of peaceful intentions: 'I just couldn't go past without admiring your lawn . . .' The resident pair open beaks and tell him off loudly, 'Ag-ag-ag-arrr!' Usually the chancer shuffles away again, but if he is very determined, he may sit for a while, head still aside. As the residents' complaints increase, he may stretch out his neck in an answering 'Ag-ag-ag-arrr!' before launching into space: after which the pair cement their delight in each other and in their garden with animated conversation and caresses.

The single egg is laid in late May, and incubated serenely by both parents in four- or five-day stints, for a full eight weeks. It takes almost as long before the downy pale grey baby is ready to fly. At first, one parent remains in attendance, but towards the end of the period the baby may be left for a day or more at a stretch, being by now practically spherical with rich feeding. It was at this stage the St Kildans made their killing. In mid-September, the parents take to the sea to recoup lost strength, and the youngsters follow as soon as fledged.

You may watch fulmars in a sunny geo for half an hour without noticing that it has other inhabitants. Look down and into the shadows, and you will almost certainly see shags. Fulmars prefer warm earthy surfaces or reflective rock in the sunshine, and a bit of vegetation for padding, but shags like cracks and crevices as dark as themselves, often against the black algae of the exposed splash zone where you would doubt a nest could survive. The nest heap, mainly of seaweed stalks, looks loose and untidy, but is painstakingly woven by the female with material brought by her mate. Later in the breeding season it is thoroughly cemented with droppings – the long trails of white below a shag's nest are usually what betray its presence. Surprisingly, these unprepossessing nests, often in clefts or caves within reach of winter waves, frequently survive to be refurbished the next year.

Watching shags on their nests is the best way to fix distinctions between shag and cormorant in the mind's eye. This is not because the two species behave very differently – they do not, and though shags tend to choose more precipitous sites, even there there is some overlap: but at the nest, they are motionless, and if you are quiet, they can be approached more closely than on the water. The shag is smaller than the goose-sized cormorant, with a more slender head and bill. There is a patch of bright yellow bare skin around the beak, but all the rest of it is black with a slight greenish sheen. The cormorant in breeding plumage has a white face and a white patch on the flank. Typically of popular bird names, the 'shag' or crest is often not in evidence except early in the breeding season.

Spend a quiet hour getting to know shags on their nests, and the young ones will still fool you: immature shags and cormorants are alike dull brown with buff underparts and a gormless expression. Size is really the only giveaway. For the last few years we have done a monthly count of dead seabirds in our area from December to March, and the most frequent casualties are always juvenile cormorants and shags. Given the size of the local populations and their inshore habits, this is not surprising, but still there is something very pathetic about these poor ungainly youngsters with their long thin necks, beaky little heads and enormous webbed feet. It is the first winter which takes toll of them; the parents are most attentive at the nest and shepherd their offspring anxiously for some time after fledging. It is very common in August to see family parties perched on the rocks, three or four callow brown young with one or both parents. Father flips in and they all flip after him, dive when he dives and fly when he flies, without, apparently, much idea at first of what it is all for. And yet this is one of the most primitive of birds, next best thing to the archaeopteryx; not much room in that tiny head for learning, you might think. But learning it must be, or they would not need parental example.

Another few weeks, and they are out in the world on their own. They stand in disconsolate rows on the skerries, thirty or forty at a time, as dismal and confused as new boys just arrived in Big School. They goggle at our passing boat with uncomprehending dismay, twisting thin necks round and almost off in search of an adult to give guidance. The class sways and gathers into little huddles of two, three or four — brothers and sisters from single nests. A chance flap of the sails, and off scurries one group of siblings, followed quickly by a two, and a three, and a four, till the whole dim-witted, bewildered company is strung out in a black V across the water. I regret every bird whose corpse is a figure on our RSPB count form, but above all I hate to find these poor brown incompetents, ungraced by rarity or beauty, yet most lovable.

Early last year I watched more breeding shags and fulmars and other birds besides than I had ever watched before. I counted and filled in forms for this body and that body, and the figures meant very little to me. I would be puzzled, deciphering my notes, to see that the morning's results consisted of two pairs of fulmars, one herring gull and three shags. Hadn't I been watching a colony? The richness and delight of the experience was a hundredfold more than these ludicrous single figures. Later in the summer I went back to Liuri (or at least to look at Liuri from as near as possible, which is not near). Suddenly, the complementary was true. That awful, unreachable, distant concavity, at the end of stark wilderness, falling to a heaving sea, had become friendly. These hundreds upon hundreds of white specks and black bristles milling and shimmering under the echoing cliffs were each a fulmar or a shag: a pair of fulmars, a family of shags, alive, at home, as thoroughly themselves here as in the little tranquil geos of Taransay or Rodel. On the way back, I noticed a blue butterfly skimming the salt-scoured clifftop, and red clover luxuriant in the lip of a blowhole. My perception had changed: Liuri remains itself.

Chapter 8

Bertie the Broad Bay Beastie
Baffles Boffins

The pretty butterfly at the edge of the cliff was a Common Blue. I had to look it up in a book. I should have known, since that is the only type of blue butterfly we get here, and I had certainly referred to that book before; but the shameful truth is that I had forgotten, if I ever knew.

Identification is an ever present problem for the amateur. Some things, however bizarre, are quite unambiguous, like the golden oriole perching forlornly in our struggling six-foot-high olearia bushes, the nearest local equivalent to a forest. Much more often, it's a case of 'What's that bird? It's a lovely bright brown with grey patches and a funny sort of crest and – oh, it's a sparrow.' Well, it's easy enough to be fooled. The sun doesn't come out here very often, and when it does, things look all sorts of strange colours, especially in the evening; and that sparrow had ecstatically fluffed up all her grey underdown to air between her feathers, and she had at some time been tonsured by a cat, which gave her a sort of tufty head. But there isn't really much excuse. Wishful thinking is awfully prevalent among would-be naturalists. All I can say in defence is that I come across some who are much worse than I am, like one knowledgeable visitor who conferred the rare status of rough-legged buzzard on a heron just because it flapped past as he was looking out of the window. I'm not sneering: repeated embarrassing mistakes have made me wary by now, but time was . . . Only last summer, my poor mother evoked red-faced tetchiness from me by telling me to 'Listen to the hawk.' The 'hawk' was in fact a displaying male golden plover. In arrogant youth, I had deduced from the moorland coincidence of that clear aerial call and 'hawks' (actually falcons: they were kestrels) that the one proceeded from the other. As self-appointed instructor to the family in matters of natural history, I had informed them accordingly. Mystery solved!

Much more recently, I had a theory about maternal care in dor beetles. Earwigs look after their eggs and hatchlings, so why not dor beetles? For once, the reference book settled matters unequivocally: 'The common dor beetle is also called the lousy watchman, as it is often infested by large numbers of parasitic mites.' So much for the tiny grey 'babies' clinging to 'mother's' abdomen!

I did learn something about the breeding arrangements of another type of beetle through the deplorable habits of Jet. All his life, Jet has had an outing every afternoon between two and three o'clock. Whatever our other commitments, Jet's walk is sacred. He is a jealous deity, and we know very well that if his rites are skimped, vengeance will swiftly follow. In his younger days, he would bring us to heel by running away from home or digging up the flower beds if his walk was delayed by half an hour. (We have never dared actually miss it out altogether.) Now, in arthritic old age when it's not so much a walk as a totter, he shows displeasure in other ways, by ripping up the car seats or piddling on the carpet. As the punishment he metes out to us has altered with changing circumstances, so has the form of his afternoon ritual. 'Walk' was never really what he had in mind: if he had merely walked, or run about, or fetched sticks on command, his human attendants might have sunk into some lethargic daydream of their own, or even into conversation with each other. Jet decided very early on that the purpose of The Walk was to direct and discipline our straying attention and focus it firmly upon His Worshipful Monstership. When he was very young, we were trained to chase him for sticks or stalks of tangle in a ritual dance which could last for an hour or more. In middle life, he would saunter to the usual limit of The Walk without a glimmer of interest in passing rabbits, until he noticed some suggestion of turning for home, when he would begin frenzied excavations. In old age, being sadly crippled, he ensures constant attentiveness by eating or pretending to eat unspeakable substances: the sort of thing he would be very offended to find in his dinner bowl, ranging from crusts of sliced white bread left by picnickers to heads of dead sheep.

Now all this may seem to have nothing to do with the family life of beetles, but consider the following. Last winter by constant vigilance I kept Monster apart from the sheep which had collapsed and died on the flat marshy field where he takes his constitutional. Yet as the mutton became more aromatic, he could be seen truffling in the grass within a 200- or 300-yard radius of it, and champing with a triumphant roll of his eyes. Whenever I managed to grab one of his treasures before he swallowed it, I found it was a little ball up to an inch in diameter of rancid tallow – there is no mistaking the smell of very old sheep's suet. I concluded that some small creature must have nibbled out these desirable lumps from the decaying corpse and trundled them off to bury against winter scarcity. I wished that Jet wouldn't destroy the careful hoard, but I'm sorry to say that these morsels remained his chief interest in life for several weeks, in spite of all my efforts to coax him outside the critical radius. I later discovered that the various burying or sexton beetles hide food in this manner. The male and female together dig under corpses of small mammals until they sink into the ground, where the flesh is gnawed into a compact ball. The female lays her eggs in a tunnel beside it, and feeds from the ball of flesh till the eggs hatch, after which she feeds the larvae on the same food regurgitated until they can fend for themselves. I suppose Jet's finds were the hard-won store of one of these types of beetle; though I never worked out why fat only was used, or why it was carried so far from the corpse. Perhaps they were gobbets dropped by birds and appropriated by the beetles. And why would the beetles be breeding so assiduously in winter? To synchronise with a seasonal glut of carrion, perhaps? Whatever the true facts, this winter so far there is no convenient dead sheep, and in spite of hopeful questing in the same marshy ground as last year, Jet has only found two carrion balls and has had to take to eating rabbit fur instead, which he doesn't like half so much.

Have I learnt something about sexton beetles or have I not? Is the fluffy yellowish stuff which grows commonly on wrack, referred to as *Leptosiphon pusillus* in Chapter 3, actually the semi-parasitic seaweed of that name? You can't produce an artistic cadence by calling it 'fluffy yellowish stuff', anyway. And what about the smallish brownish goose I saw on Shillay in July? A Canada goose – no, its whole face was white. A barnacle, then. No – too brown. A *young* barnacle? Should have been in Greenland at the time. Canada then: no, scarce in Scotland except on ornamental lakes in parks, no ornamental lakes on oceanic Shillay! Barnacle that thought Shillay was very like Greenland, fooled by climate. Should have said 'gnuk'. It didn't, it said 'aangk' very clearly. What do Canadas say? 'Aa-honk.'

And so on. I have seen plenty of Canada geese on ornamental lakes in parks, and a fair number of barnacles barking overhead in winter, yet I still can't tell which that unexpected single bird was. It was just the same with the killer whales we saw, after years of wishing to see whales. They porpoised along, twice the length of our boat, with wonderful fins like female killers, and just the right sort of expression, but they didn't have (or at least we didn't see) the diagnostic white patches every photograph of killers clearly shows: yet they didn't look the least like anything else, unless perhaps false killer whales, *Orca pseudorca*? 'Identification is usually very easy ... the teeth are unmistakable ... circular in cross-section [the killer whale's are oval.]' Oh. I didn't look at the teeth. To tell the truth I was pretty scared to see the enormous smirking head surging at us broadside on, and very glad when it went under us without a ripple. I don't think I would have wanted to see any teeth. I *had* observed that every seal had vanished from the area, maybe that had something to do with noticing the teeth were oval? Perhaps I'm just a total coward. Perhaps they weren't twice the length of *Sand Eel*, perhaps just half the length – pilot whales? Risso's dolphins? And what noise did they make? How often did they blow? I didn't see them blow at all – hopeless! I know they crackled with the might and power of Leviathan, but after ten minutes at the reference books, I wonder if I dreamt it all.

Conditions in the field seldom allow the observations necessary to pin down a species you have never seen before: at least not in the Hebrides. The weather is often simply vile, so that even using binoculars may be impossible, but even when this isn't the case, the lack of easily measurable items such as houses or trees makes distance, and therefore size, difficult to gauge. Then our light is very shifting, slanting, dim or iridescent depending on time of year and time of day. I have stared at picture after picture of cetaceans sporting in calm, sunlit water, in the Arctic, in the Antarctic, in Florida, and the rest of the world looks very unlike the Hebrides. Even on a good day (and it was a fine July midday when we saw the killer or not-killer whales) there is usually haze in the sky, movement in the water, reflection and shadow leaping from wave to wave. It takes very long familiarity to make quick positive identification from a moving boat in that sort of light.

On a rough day, it becomes virtually impossible to identify anything you don't already know by heart. Every year we see small groups of dapper black-ended, white-middled ducks bobbing around in the Sound in late summer. 'Late summer' is often something of a euphemism: by mid-August weather is frequently chilly and turbulent. For some time we had argued viciously over what these ducks were – tufted, scaup or goldeneye. One day we took a pocket bird book with us to make certain. You might think we would have done this before: but what with water out of the sea, water out of the sky, and water running down our arms on to the pages, books are not practical in-boat entertainment. We took our tattiest one, in a polythene bag. I sucked my fingers to dry them and get the circulation back before introducing them carefully into the bag to turn pages. We beat out into the lumpy tide-race behind Jane's Tower, bucking and slamming in the steep confused chop of wind against tide. The wind is always against the tide: it is my opinion that the wind changes when the tide does, just to be against it again, and I hold to this as firmly as Pliny to the belief that the dead corpse of a man floateth upon the water with the face upward, but contrariwise women swim grovelling. On this occasion, the wind was so much against the tide and the distinction between rain and spray so blurred that I began to have a presentiment about swimming grovelling, and whimpered to go home; but a momentary lull between squalls revealed that our ducks were still there, bobbing nonchalantly up and down in the hissing grey water between us and the shore. We turned off the wind towards them, and came within a couple of boatlengths – about thirty feet or so. I kept my drier hand in the polythene bag and brushed away globs of water with the other.

'Scaup, definitely.'

'No! they haven't got grey backs.'

'They've fluffed up the white bits.'

'They've got a mark near the eye, must be goldeneye.'

'I can't see any mark. That one's got a sort of crest.'

'It's just the way it's ruffling its feathers.'

So it went on. The jaunty birds zoomed up and down the steep waves, appearing and disappearing with about the same frequency as a child on a pogoball. We trailed them for twenty minutes, and never seemed to see them for more than a second at a time. Binoculars are useless in a rough sea – you find you are at the top of a wave staring fixedly at the sky while your subject is down in a trough, and every crash of the boat catches you unawares and threatens you with a broken nose. The ducks were unconcerned. They turned this way and that, fluffed up now the white and now the black, stretched their necks to goose length and contracted them to nothing, erected crests out of nowhere and stuck out tails and wings at angles never seen in bird books. We have never been closer to ducks except at a park duckpond, yet we still haven't decided what they were. The only bird we positively identified that day was a smew. It looked more like the picture in the book than any duck I have ever seen. The only trouble is, it shouldn't have been there at all: smews are about as rare in this area as rough-legged buzzards.

We do get rarities, of course, drifted in on currents and blown in on storms. The oddest we ever came across, though not a personal discovery, was found at Ness in Lewis. A Lewisman rang up and asked to speak to Andrew. I am always suspicious of men who don't seem inclined to divulge the purpose of their call to other men's wives; I therefore eavesdropped on one side of a conversation which went something like this: 'That's very interest-ing . . . ah-really, I don't know if I can be of any help, though . . . well, yes . . . I used to, but only small things, dead birds and so on . . . borax, you get it from the chemist. I might have some, but you'll probably need more . . . no really, I think it would be too big a job for me. I'm pretty busy – sorry . . . look, if you can't find anyone else to have a go . . .'

The Ness fishermen's co-operative, it seemed, were in possession of a turtle hauled up dead in a fishing net. They wanted someone with a knowledge of taxidermy to stuff it, so that it could be kept as a curio. Andrew, in spite of his disclaimers, obviously rather fancied stuffing a turtle. Magnanimously, I gave my consent. He consulted his book on taxidermy and rang the fishermen's co-op in Ness to tell them he'd be right over. He came away from the telephone grey and shaking.

'He said they're bringing it down here.'

'What? I don't want it here! You're not stuffing it in the kitchen! Why on earth didn't you tell him you'd do it up there?'

'They've got it loaded up already.'

'Well, they could unload it.'

'It's – I think they've had quite a job with it. They've got it on a tractor and trailer.'

I stared.

'How big is it?' I asked at last.

Andrew was unwilling to admit it. 'About seven feet long. It weighs . . . er . . . quite a bit.'

My consent was withdrawn at once. I think the Ness fishermen managed to cram the thing into their industrial freezer, to await some more accomplished taxidermist with a more accommodating wife.

The creature was a leatherback turtle, the largest type, and this was a big one, weighing about half a ton. The leatherback's carapace is formed of longitudinally ridged plates *under* the skin, unlike that of other turtles, which have hard shells outside the body. This streamlined, elongated back, together with immensely strong foreflippers, make it the fastest swimmer, but nevertheless it usually keeps within its tropical home range. Why this one had followed the cooling Gulf Stream as far north as the Butt of Lewis is a mystery, though they do follow swarms of jellyfish, their principal food.

The leatherback could be decisively identified because of its peculiar carapace. It is, in fact, sole living representative of the order Dermochelyidae. Somehow that is reassuring: there's nothing like putting a name to something to make you feel you know what it's all about. Children delight in the naming process; Sarah would prattle about Bird's Foot Trefoil and Bog Pimpernel almost before she could walk, and under the influence of a cousin a few years older, soon bewildered us with Sea Potatoes, Pea Urchins, Thin Tellins and Octopus Jellyfish. The Octopus Jellyfish (which is, as you would expect, a jellyfish which looks remarkably like an octopus) was almost a cause of mental breakdown in my brother. On a summer visit, they had taken the foot-ferry to North Uist, and the boat was surrounded by whales – unidentifiable, of course.

My brother, overwhelmed by the awe and beauty of these creatures, tried to convey to the children the wonder of what they were seeing. They took no notice: they were counting jellyfish. Why bother with an indeterminate number of whales which you cannot name, when you are surrounded by jellyfish which you can both name and count? To this day, the children have no recollection of the whales, but they do remember that they saw 153 jellyfish, of which four were Octopus Jellyfish.

We are all children when it comes to naming names. I have seen a good scholarly case made out for the artistry of the Catalogue of the Ships in the *Iliad*, but I don't believe it. The thing is a total yawn, a lazy, infantile, nonsensical piece of babbling, concocted by a nodding Homer for a regressive, thumbsucking audience who had probably had too much to drink. We love names, we pile them up, we gloat over them, we imagine they cast a spell on the world and place it in our hands to play with: a dangerous superstition, conducive to mental sloth. Consider Tom Lehrer's Harvard man summing up the table of the elements, and with it the secrets of the universe:

'These are the only ones of which the news has come to Harvard; There may well be some others, but they haven't been discovered.'

– and what we don't know isn't knowledge.

All the same, I wish I knew how to name these whales. And what about Bertie the Broad Bay Beastie? He evoked a memorable headline in the *Stornoway Gazette* – so memorable that I have entirely forgotten what he was. I know he was badly decomposed and thus rendered baffling, as well as smelly; and that whatever he had been, by the time he was Bertie he had become news to the *Gazette* reporter, delight to passing dogs, and dinner to the blackbacks.

Chapter 9

Where Have All the Whales Gone?

The answer is: into street lights, umbrellas, corsets, chronometers; soap, margarine, lipstick, glue; pharmaceuticals, fertilisers, petfoods, nuclear warheads; up the spout, down the drain. All this is well known. The unexpected thing, given the sort of animals that we are, is that the question makes so many of us in the Western world feel guilty, even if we have rigorously excluded suspect petfoods and cosmetics from our personal shopping lists for years. Why should we, who are not whalers or even citizens of whaling nations, feel not only regret but shame for the decline of the whales?

Two hundred, a hundred, even fifty years ago, public opinion was quite different. 'Our whaling fleet may be said at this day to whiten the Pacific with its canvas, and the proceeds of this fishery give comfort and happiness to many thousands of our citizens,' wrote American Lt Charles Wilkes in 1845; and in Archibald Thorburn's *British Mammals* of 1920, the entries for cetaceans are more to do with whaling than whales, admiration being reserved for the 'brave and hardy' boat crews and the consequent 'profit'. How has this undeniable 'profit' come to seem an obscenity in the eyes of so many people?

The respectable, public reason for concern, the reason always given by politicians and economists and bodied forth in the official pronouncements of the International Whaling Commission, is 'declining stocks'. *Stocks*, notice: implying a resource which may, wisely used, still produce a profit. But if you ask private individuals why they think whales should not be hunted, more likely answers are 'It's cruel', 'They're too intelligent', 'They're so peaceful'.

All these reasons, public and private, stand up to examination. There is no doubt at all that nearly every cetacean species from common porpoise to blue whale is in dramatic decline. Many of the smaller toothed whales – porpoises, dolphins, pilot and killer whales – suffer not only from direct hunting, but from the extermination programmes of competing fishermen, incidental kill in fishing nets, and disturbance by engine noise of their vital echolocatory functions. Nevertheless, the best documented declines are among the baleen whales and the only large toothed whale, the sperm; in other words, among those species which were or are commercially profitable. In 1823, when the fishery of bowheads off eastern Canada was already flagging for want of prey, a ship's log could report in one day's voyage 'along the floe edge the dead bodies of hundreds of flenched whales ... towards evening the numbers come across were ever increasing.' These were *crangs*, the corpses jettisoned after the whalers had stripped blubber and baleen. Today the world population of bowheads is unlikely to be more than 3000. Protection came in 1937, but probably too late to save the species.

Arctic whaling had become commercially unviable long before that, and attention switched to the southern oceans. In 1867, the explosive harpoon was invented. Less than a hundred years later, there were so few great whales left that restraints had to be agreed if there were to be any left to kill. At the same time, the petroleum industry and its by-products had rendered many whale products unnecessary, at least to the nations which didn't eat whale and could afford to be self-righteous about it. If markets had still been as good, one suspects that every species of baleen whale would have been hunted to extinction regardless. Even after forty years of varying degrees of protection, population numbers are still precariously low: blue whales, the largest animals ever seen on earth, are estimated at 13,000, greys, beloved of whale-watchers, at 15,000, the singing humpback at a pathetic 2500. Bryde's, sei and fin whales, though also numbered only in thousands, are still hunted. Even sperm whales, estimated at 1½ million, are scarcely thriving, bearing in mind that in the 1960s the catch of sperms was 2900 *per year*.

This isn't simply some juggling with figures to do with far-off Antarctica. While the great whales have dwindled from millions to thousands, older inhabitants of coastal communities even in Britain can remember the large herds of smaller cetaceans, particularly porpoises, which used to be commonly encountered. Here, we see porpoises now singly or in twos and threes, if at all. Ten years ago in the same areas one seldom saw fewer than ten at a time; and fifty years ago they came in their hundreds, rolling through the Sound in pursuit of herring. They must have competed with the fishermen, but they are remembered and regretted for the drama and beauty of their chase. And not only porpoises: every summer the killer whales came, surging up into the shallow water after fish and seals. 'I've seen them leaping there right in among the moorings', we were told by a fisherman friend who is a knowledgeable observer of wildlife: he was pointing about thirty yards off shore from Leverburgh pier. Meanwhile, in the north of Harris, Lord Leverhulme had injected capital into the whaling station at Buonavoneader, which supplied the necessary for Sunlight Soap. The quarry was plentiful, taken on the migratory route along the 200-metre line west of St Kilda, blue, sperm and northern right whales. The stinking plume of smoke from the rendering boilers is still remembered by half the population of the island. Then there are the numerous accounts of beachings and strandings, arguing a much larger cetacean population than now swims in Hebridean waters. Fewer of everything: fewer lobsters, prawns, herring, mackerel; fewer porpoises, dolphins, whales; fewer in-shore fishermen. More big boats from far away with implacable sonar and mile after mile of monofilament: inimical to traditional fishing communities in a way the porpoises and orca never were. Everyone feels the draining of life from the seas, as they must on every coast in the northern hemisphere. Decline is not merely a page of statistics.

As to intelligence, for which the whales, especially the dolphins and killers, have had such a good press in the last twenty years, there are now enough careful experimental results to convince all but a few diehards in scientific circles that the large brains of cetaceans are actually *brainy*. In particular, the complex audible signals emitted by dolphins and killers have been grudgingly admitted to be a form of communication akin to human language in subtlety. This has become more difficult to deny as the astonishing ability of captive dolphins to understand and respond to human speech has been documented, and as wild killer whales have been discovered to possess tribal 'dialects', a specialisation previously thought to be possible only for human language. Similarly astounding was the discovery that male humpback whales on the breeding grounds produce long and very complicated 'songs', different for each individual, which resound across a whole ocean and communicate even to a human a great deal of information about the singer. The suspicion that some cetaceans are capable of language has done a lot for our estimate of whale intelligence: as addicted language-users ourselves, we tend to assume no intelligence without language, rather as a Celtic fan assumes no football without his team. Indeed so fixed is faith in the reciprocal relationship of language and intelligence that a fanatical few try constantly to redefine what language is, so that it can be denied to other animals: the fear being, presumably, that if language is allowed them, intelligence must be too – and then how would we justify the human race? It is, in fact, far from settled that intelligence (or consciousness, or awareness – whatever vague special 'something' it is we wish other animals didn't have) cannot exist without language; but undoubtedly the equation has put whales up in everyone's estimation.

Peacefulness is evident in the social relationships of all cetaceans, wild or captive. Some, particularly the sperm whale, spar for mates, and others, particularly dolphins, for group dominance; but on the whole they are remarkably co-operative and gentle with each other. In some species, midwives assist the baby to take its first breath, and mother's helps babysit thereafter. Nursing mother humpbacks are often escorted and protected by an adult male. Among grey whales, mating is a friendly *ménage à trois*, with a second male obligingly propping the happy couple in position during their embraces. The more that is learned about whale behaviour, the more their reputation for peacefulness seems warranted. In fact, they would be unlikely to be crotchety animals: being powerful, free-swimming, and slow breeding, they have never faced competition for living space or food. They had no enemies before man. They may well have evolved as creatures incapable of fury, or even self-defence.

So the whales are declining, they are intelligent, they are peaceful. It needs no Moby Dick come from the grave to tell us that: it has all been known for centuries. When they had hunted the Arctic whales to near extinction, the whalers turned gleeful attentions to the newly-reported herds of the Antarctic. No one felt remorse for the bowhead, any more than for the dodo or the great auk. Ethnic populations took care not to overhunt, out of prudent regard for the future; not so civilised man, scouring the globe in his fast-moving fleets, confident of God on his side. It was in the natural order of things that Providence should shower successive bounties on his deserving people. Reckless expansionism of every sort was sanctioned by western Christianity: the Gospel was to be carried to all lands, and it was only to be expected that the races considered by the Almighty superior enough to convey it should be amply rewarded by the natural riches of the rest of the world. In four centuries of escalating religious and political arrogance, white Christians plundered the globe, wiping out 350 species and sub-species of birds and mammals, destroying and demoralising millions of indigenous humans. 'I thank thee, O Lord. Thou alone hast done all,' wrote Svend Foyn in his diary the day he patented the explosive harpoon: as it happened, it was Christmas Eve.

We should not imagine that these our recent ancestors, who brought the American Indian, the bison, the blue whale, the Australian aborigine to the verge of extinction, were either fanatical religious bigots or unfeeling vandals. Simply, they were raised in a confident religious and moral tradition which gave them sure values – values which so obviously succeeded in bringing home the goods that hardly anyone questioned them, any more than most of us today would question the value of literacy or women's votes. Again and again in the accounts of the old whalers (and sometimes even in the accounts of the South Sea missionaries) there is a note of pity for what is being destroyed. 'There is something extremely painful in the destruction of a whale, when thus evincing a degree of affectionate regard for its offspring which would do honour to the superior intelligence of human beings; yet the object of the adventure, the value of the prize, the joy of the capture cannot be sacrificed to feelings of compassion.' Thus wrote William Scoresby in 1820, of an occasion when a mother whale remained by her infant till six harpoons killed her, 'in the course of an hour.' His assurance that compassion is secondary and even misleading reads very like the earlier exhortations of the Dominicans or Jesuits not to pity heretics put to the torture or the stake; or for that matter, like the similar protestations of present-day vivisectionists that sympathy for experimental animals is misplaced. Unfortunately, the old Adam is not dead yet.

Looking at humanity's failings kindly, one can see that people need social values, that it is almost impossible to stand outside the morality of one's own age and place; in a more cynical mood, one may feel that the dominant ethic known to humanity is always and only convenience. In the great age of whaling, the hunters knew as well as any modern whale-watcher that whales are intelligent creatures, loyal and peaceful in their relations to each other, and even in their attitude to men. Stories of drowning humans rescued by dolphins and eyewitness accounts of friendly whales rubbing against boats before they were harpooned were commonplace for centuries. Indeed, cetacean gentleness was exploited by whalers. Drive one pilot whale ashore and the rest will follow its cries of alarm – a method used a century or so ago in Lewis, and to this day in the Faeroes. An injured sperm whale kept close to the ship will attract all its comrades within hearing range, a radius of about six miles. Capture an infant whale of any species, and certainly its mother, usually other adults too, will come to assist it. These horrors were all made possible because the whales were co-operative enough to respond to each other's distress, and so docile that they would scarcely ever defend themselves, let alone attack their aggressors. The decline, the intelligence and the peacefulness of whales were not sudden discoveries of the 1950s: the whole whaling industry was designed to exploit them.

So what has changed? One must beware of hailing a new dawn of human sensibility: one very pragmatic change is that the Western world now hardly needs the whale. Man-made substitutes will perform as well as whale products except for finest grade machine oil got from sperm whales, which is mainly used in weaponry. Its import is prohibited in many countries, though by all accounts there is still a black market in it, as there is in plutonium; but at least it is a cheering sign that, as with that other war-directed product, governments are afraid to admit the trade occurs. To bring this about, the message that whales should not be hunted must have gone surprisingly deep. It has affected even Iceland, a traditional whaling nation which depends heavily on fisheries: the last public opinion poll taken there showed a majority against whaling, and the powerful Women's Party opposes it. The Russians seem resigned to the eventual end of whaling. Only the

Japanese are unaffected by the western orgy of guilt and remorse. They have ended up puzzled and offended: the minke whale which is their main catch now is thriving and in no danger of extinction, yet international disapproval grows apace. In vain for them to point out that they use every bit of every whale they catch, which is more than western whalers ever did. In worldwide public opinion, all whaling stinks. The IWC's official talk of sustainability, resource management and building up stocks is a front: what actually counts is that enormous numbers of people find the concept of whalehunting as revolting as cannibalism. Now that we no longer depend for 'comfort and happiness' on whale products, the ethic of convenience can be pushed out of the way.

But what is materially convenient and what is spiritually satisfying are intricately related in any given age. The prosperity of the expansionist era was a sign of God's favour. His privileged darlings were free, from Eden onwards, to use, plunder and torment the natural world, like spoilt brats teasing the family puppy. How has it come about that in the latter half of this century we are not so sure he is pleased with us after all? What has produced the shift in spiritual consciousness which puts man in the bad boy's corner, and God on the side of the whales?

In the past hundred years or so, we have twice had our heads held over the abyss: once by Darwin's evolutionary theory, and once by the atomic bomb. From the first we pulled back kicking and struggling, to the second we rushed with imbecilic delight. Two terrible glimpses of the human spirit fit like the pieces of a jigsaw. We are not God's chosen favourites, inheritors of the earth now and of glory forever, but a disruptive, chaotic, catastrophic blip in the latest second of universal time; perhaps in the last second, for we play unthinkingly with the weapons of Ragnarok. The picture is so terrifying that more than a century after Darwin, we are still trying to pin the pages together so that we needn't look: so that the wilful ignorance of fundamentalist religion is not losing, but gaining ground today, with the let-out of eternal life after death beckoning the saved towards a nuclear Judgment Day. Even apart from this extreme reaction, the import of evolutionary theory could not penetrate childish conceit until with nuclear fission we had contrived something so appallingly delinquent as to wake a nightmare fear that we are not worthy to imagine ourselves as lords of creation: and having come to doubt that, insofar as we have, we can now look back through time and see what furious, fractious infants we have been. Not much wonder if we turn for inspiration to the whales, who were singing and talking and loving each other millions of years before the first hominids started braining their neighbours.

Sweeping claims, maybe. Common sense demurs that the whales aren't saints, that they aren't even all the same sort of creature. Some species are mostly brain, some are mostly blubber; some are solitary and some are sociable; some are only nice to their family group, some seem benevolent all round. And all are carnivorous: every whale species from the krill-sifting baleen whales to the seal-eating killer devours other living creatures in order to survive. They are only mild because they don't need to be fierce; they have evolved that way to fit the available ecological niche. Their social arrangements are interesting, but paralleled in other animals, attributable to the drive for genetic survival rather than to high-flown altruism.

But when we have levelled the worst criticisms we can against the whales, in the end we have to fall silent, ashamed. Peaceful, intelligent. What in human history has been both peaceful and intelligent? If there is any room for optimism in viewing the human condition today, it is surely to be found in that shame. The only glimmer of hope for the planet is for humanity to feel shame, not only before the whales, but before all Nature.

Chapter 10

Gales, Geese

The first gale of autumn this year was on the second of September. Knowing it would be our last chance for the year, we had taken advantage of a light wind in the morning against a favourable tide to beat down to grim Dunaarin, at the Minch end of the Sound. I wanted to see whether the white patches on the black which I had spotted earlier from neighbouring Gilsay were shag sites.

'Calmest day we've ever been round here. You could almost land,' remarked Andrew, as we eased off between Cleit an Duin and the imposing green-topped pile of Dunaarin itself. He always says that, to forestall my nervous jittering about the place. I was on the point of agreeing when we hit the usual sickening swell which humps over the jagged rocks on the west corner and prowls and pushes up the bare cliffs facing the Minch. It was obvious before we rounded to look up at these cliffs that no shags could have nested there: even on that calm morning, a short confused swell was lifting and falling fifteen feet at the foot of the precipice. The white splashes were smears of bleached algae. A few late fulmars banked past us, heading for their fast-depopulating ledges on the more hospitable side – if sentinel Dunaarin could ever be called hospitable. Two marooned rams gazed forlornly at us from the tiny lush guano pasture on the top. They had been left there to get fit and fat for a November harem, though how they could be caught and removed without accident was a puzzle. A seal rolled at the base of the cliffs, at ease in the gathering water. It watched us with mild eyes as we pitched and slammed in every swell and rebound.

Our sailing forays are usually decided for us by direction of wind and current. We nearly always sail to windward on the way out, so that if the wind freshens we can enjoy an exciting reach or run home, rather than a reefed, wet, miserable beat. Since the currents run so strongly in the Sound, in all but a very fresh – rather too fresh – breeze, it is impossible to make headway against both wind *and* tide, so that our choice is often directed to wind-across-tide routes. Better still is to time the expedition to allow for the tide turning, so that it is favourable both ways, but in practice this rarely works out. The tidal streams in the Sound are extraordinarily complicated. In summer, at neaps, they run in from the Atlantic for twelve hours, approximately from six am to six pm, and out from the Minch for the other twelve. In winter, the direction is reversed. This doesn't look too bad on paper, and even seems to be correct for about four days a month during ten months of the year; but the rest of the time it's never quite clear till you hit the stream whether it is more neaps than springs, more summer than winter, more day than night, or the other way about. There are so many narrow channels and reefs that unpredictable back-eddies can turn the current head to tail, so that it is not unknown to see the float of a lobster pot taut on its rope heading south-east in the main stream, while a rope and float fifteen yards away strain in the opposite direction. Sailing tactics which exploit wind and tide are very rewarding when they succeed, but unfortunately about half the time they don't. Wind can drop or change direction as easily as freshen, and the tides remain a source of perplexity.

These particulars on sailing strategy are not actually a build up to a heroic maritime drama. I am reminded of a story I once heard (from a mainland Scot, of course) illustrating the peculiarities of the Hebridean narrative style. A venerable island fisherman, with the faraway look and rhetorical skill of his race, was relating a long and intricate tale of a trip in a small boat with an English chentleman as passenger. When due eloquence had been paid to the lowering skies, the towering waves, the uproar of many waters, the growing despair of the English chentleman, the narrator paused, fixing his riveted audience with a sombre and bardic eye. After a mind-tingling silence came the punch line, delivered with sepulchral emphasis: 'And the English chentleman leaned over the side . . . and he wass sick!'

Just as eventful was our sail back from Dunaarin. For once, wind and tide behaved predictably. As we turned up channel on to a comfortable broad reach, the wind freshened delightfully, still against the tide, but in sufficiently slack water to promote exhilaration rather than terror. The wind continued to strengthen rapidly and to back, so that we surged home on a tremendous run, flying over a sea of vivid glass green already streaking with foam.

Spray rainbows burst from our bows; the air was full of white birds hurrying to sheltered water ahead of the storm, fulmars, snowy kittiwakes, sparkling shearwaters, against a steel blue sky. We rushed on through the moorings under full sail, missing drying reefs and parked boats by a hairsbreadth, turned gallantly up into wind, and misjudged our buoy by two feet for no good reason whatsoever. But at least no one wass sick.

The gale that night was not particularly severe, no worse than on several days in the previous month. Yet somehow it defined the end of summer. It is always the same with the first storm of September: even though bland days may follow, milder and calmer than our often dismal July and August weather, the threat of winter is openly abroad. From our front windows at home, the sun no longer sets into the sea, but behind the dark summit of Chaipaval, firing its familiar bulk with illusory volcanic splendour. Daylight recedes and slants towards the equinox, nights lose the lingering summer afterglow, the Northern Lights pale and shift again above the distant mountains. It is a time of great beauty, of baroque cloudscapes, brilliant rainbows and resplendent heather tints on the hills, but it is not a season I love. In a land without trees, the decline of the year proceeds starkly, without the gradual mellowness of russet and yellow mainland autumn. The garden flowers and the remaining wild ones too are battered by the first salt-laden gales and don't find heart to rise again. There are no harvest fields: the nearest approximations are the few crofts with fences still festooned in wet blackening hay set there to 'dry', soon to be joined by even less likely wisps of green oats. The only other crop is potatoes. Sometimes on a sunny calm day, the smell of these newly dug is a real scent of autumn, a nostalgic reminder of a state that has never existed here, rustic well-being in the enjoyment of earth's plenty. The land here could produce far more than it does today, but even with all the harsh toil of the past, its human population never reaped bountifully, never lived other than precariously, on the edge of dearth and winter all their lives.

When summer is past, it is not autumn, but the forecourt of winter. The birds are on the move, with great flocks of lapwings, golden plover and curlews sweeping over the moors and saltings. The breeding cliffs and islands are deserted, even by the latest fulmars. Everything is strangely quiet; family parties have broken up, so that even the soft contact calls of parents and young which succeed the hubbub of the nesting season have ceased. An occasional young gull still mews persistently at its parents, but it can mew all day, and they will not respond; the business at hand now for all the adults is survival, to feed as much as possible and build up the fat reserves depleted during the strenuous work of breeding, in order to combat the coming rigours of cold, darkness and scarcity. The young must take their chance; for the late broods, it is not a good one.

To the human observer, the young seem pathetic at this stage, and the parent birds heartless or witless, depending on the individual's view of avian capability. The biologist will correctly point out that to maximise the survival of a species, the adults must invest massive effort in rearing young to a certain viable stage, which in the case of most birds is at fledging. Thereafter, time and energy are more profitably used to ensure their own fitness for the next breeding season: it would be throwing good money after bad to bolster up unviable runts, and the fact that only the fittest juveniles will survive to breed is of ultimate benefit to the species.

Well, the biologist can afford to take this God's-eye view (though there isn't, of course, any proof that God thinks in the cool economic metaphors so fashionable with biologists at the moment). But how do the birds feel about the dismal, ruffled, begging offspring they are studiously ignoring, except when they drive it away in a sudden spasm of anger? Has their erstwhile parental devotion been soothed out of existence by the convincing statistics of the divine economist? Are they so stupid they simply don't recognise their children any more? Are they such reflexive automata that the new plumage of offspring once they fledge is enough to provoke aggression rather than nurturing?

Probably none of these simplifications is totally untrue. But before concluding that any of them is totally true, I think we should consider some human stories. In pre-Revolutionary Russia, it was common for peasant women to have newborn infants baptised, and then leave them to die of starvation: only in that way could the mother be freed for the heavy work necessary for survival. By baptism, she did what she could, in such harsh circumstances, for the child, and then turned her back on a bad business. Then consider the many European folk tales of the Hansel and Gretel or Molly Whuppie type. These stories begin with a peasant family so poor that the only chance of survival for the parents is to 'lose' the children far away from home. In most versions of the story the children are left with some food, and reassurances about coming back later: the parents are depicted as bowing to necessity, not as committing a heinous crime.

In our own time and place, it is by no means uncommon to hear parents justifying themselves with reassurances such as 'We've done all we can for her', 'We've given him a good start in life', 'We really can't afford to do any more'. Such plaints usually indicate parents who are trying to sever ties of responsibility they still feel, rightly or wrongly, for full-grown offspring who are perceived to be in some sort of trouble, whether emotional, moral or material. No one is much surprised when sorely-tried human parents wash their hands thus of hopeless black sheep who have run off with other people's spouses or cars, taken to drugs or drink, developed Aids, or failed their exams for the third time. We may feel such young are pathetic, but their parents are under duress – and to be frank – didn't we always think that boy wasn't quite right, that girl was a bad lot?

We are back, in fact, to the unviable runts. In our secure and well-fed Western lives, we can afford to keep our runts going – up to a certain cut-off point. The parents of Hansel and Gretel couldn't afford to keep going so long: poor Russian peasants even less. I don't mean to claim that the herring gulls in our field are living under a crushing burden of guilt for the care they can no longer afford to lavish on their offspring; but most human parents who have made the hand-washing decision don't collapse under the pangs of conscience either, they simply try to get on with life. The God's-eye overview of their activities in relation to species survival would be much the same for birds and humans. *We* know, of course, the emotional content of rearing (and rejecting) offspring among our own species. Because we *do* know it, we should not assume that other animals lack it, allowing them only the basic species survival formula – which applies as well to us as to them. The great ethologist Konrad Lorenz quotes his admired teacher

Otto Heinroth, whose analyses were thought by objectors to deny animals feelings, 'On the contrary, I regard animals as very emotional people with very little intelligence!' The point is worth considering. No bird or animal couple sits down to a rational discussion of family planning with due regard to both the state of the species at this moment in time and the investment of effort which they as individuals can responsibly afford. A number of human couples do just this: and since they nearly always decide that their own offspring are bound to be brighter, bigger and better than anyone else's, they usually go on to produce far too many anyway – in other words, like everyone else, they subordinate reason to emotion when their personal lives are touched. Emotion is what keeps life going: if it didn't seem pleasurable and satisfying to do so, no animals, including ourselves, would court, copulate, eat, drink or be merry. In the end it's being merry that counts: and that cannot be unless there is love for what you are doing. We should forget about love being a refined human capacity: it is a basic biological cement. We have no reason to suppose that the sexton beetles instinctively burying their ball of carrion are not totally infatuated with the task, in a fair passion of fulfilment and satisfaction, rejoicing in doing the one thing in the universe it seems right to do: *loving* it! If they didn't, why would they bother? They lack language to express it, they lack memory and foresight to integrate it with other acts and times, but it is unlikely they lack the strong, stark, compelling emotion itself.

Of course, in our own species, it is by expressing, communicating, remembering, anticipating that we weave the stuff of our emotional lives. The raw material is left behind in earliest infancy: the newborn baby in a paroxysm of starving rage or blissfully full at the breast knows only the intense, primary emotion of the sexton beetle.

Heinroth and Lorenz both spent years studying the greylag goose, a bird whose emotions are so like our own in equivalent situations that few people would fail to recognise the fact, once it was pointed out – but it took Heinroth to point it out, and Lorenz to popularise it, before a human public could see what was to be seen. Goose-shooting sportsmen presumably still do not know, or (worse and scarcely credible) do not care, that the affectional bonds of all geese, and particularly greylags, can be lifelong. Greylags pair for life, usually after an infatuated youthful courtship. The bond is not primarily sexual: the most important expression of it is shared 'triumph calling', which also keeps siblings and parents and children together. Geese who have triumph-called together are united for life; and though young unpaired geese or the occasional adulterer may copulate outside 'marriage', the triumph calling which follows mating of spouses never takes place in these casual situations. A greylag which has lost its mate will grieve commonly for a year and often for life, and when bereft may return to its parents, even though during 'marriage' it has appeared to have lost all recognition of them. The family bond is very strong: the gander will defend his mate and brood to the death if necessary, and the fledged young spend at least their first winter with their parents.

Lorenz describes the intense experience which first drew him as a very small boy to the geese: 'I heard above me some metallic calls, and then saw, way up in the sky, a flock of wild geese heading downstream . . . I can still relive today what I felt at that moment. I did not know where the birds were flying, but I wanted to migrate with them. I was filled with a romantic, chest-expanding, heart-bursting longing to travel.' It was a reaction of pure untutored emotion to this most emotional of creatures, a direct, electric current of feeling. I think it is a common enough response: even the strange people who persist in shooting geese often describe the arrival of their quarry out of a winter dawn in terms of near mystical rapture.

Few people can resist searching the sky for geese when they hear these voices, and if you look at upturned faces as the skein passes, you will see wonder, delight and love even in features which seldom show such softening. Why geese should have this instant effect on humans is a mystery. They are not the only migratory birds or the most musical or beautiful. Some farmers even learn to regard them as vermin. Yet there can hardly be a bird with greater emotive value, unless perhaps the first cuckoo of spring.

By 'geese' in our part of the world I mean greylags. We see occasional small groups of barnacles barking high overhead, but the geese who straggle southward, exhausted in an autumn sunset, so that they make you cry, who knife joyfully northward in a blue spring morning, so that they make you cry again, who fly off calling anxiously when the accustomed solitude of their islets is invaded, who waddle peacefully across the dim winter marsh — even then they make you cry! At least they make *me* cry: the ponderous feet and portly fluffy backsides of a greylag family grazing the ditches tightens my throat more reliably than Shakespeare's finest hour. I have no difficulty in believing in the emotional intensity of goosey life.

Most wild greylags are migratory, birds of the sub-arctic. Many thousands winter in Britain, which also has a resident feral population, but the only truly wild native birds, a mere 200 or so pairs, live year-round in the west of Scotland and the Hebrides, most of them in South Uist. Indeed, reference books often deny any breeding pairs to the Harris area and it has been one of our happiest birdwatching experiences to realise that this is no longer true. On many of the small uninhabited islands, small flocks of greylags, up to about thirty birds at a time, can be found grazing on the green vegetation, which tends to be lusher there than on the overgrazed mainland of Harris. But a nesting situation looks quite different even from a long way off. On the crown of an island, you may spot the silhouette of a watchful gander, neck upright and alert. Though plainly anxious about the approaching boat, he will not fly away or call, and may even come a little nearer, to have a closer look. Then he hurries off on foot, as fast and as inconspicuously as is possible for a stout grey bird on a small green island with no cover. As he disappears over the ridge, another head and neck may appear beside his, and with any luck, three or four smaller ones in between, and off they all waddle, father in front and mother behind, scrambling and slipping on the weedy rocks, till the whole family are afloat in a long line. This secretive manoeuvre is concluded without a cackle or a flap, unlike most goose business.

We hope that these isolated families are pioneers spreading out from the tiny nucleus of native greylags on South Uist, and that in years to come more geese will nest on the sweet lush islands of the Sound. Against this hope, some years ago there were geese nesting on the large island of Taransay off the west of Harris. Feral mink attacked them, killing geese as they sat on their eggs. Not surprisingly, they have ceased to use that island; and we have noticed that though they love to graze the delightful grassy islets of Saghay Bheag and Saghay Mhor, they don't nest there: these too are infested by mink.

In the clear spaces between the autumn gales, the Icelandic geese come through like heroes, calling encouragement to each other, sometimes resting a night on the Northton saltmarsh, sometimes flying on low over the isthmus there and out across the Sound to their wintering grounds further south. I often wonder what our little population of residents make of their splendour and clamour. Perhaps sometimes an adventurous young Hebridean gander is caught up in the excitement, and goes a-viking to the stubble fields of the south, winning at last (one hopes) the respect of the strangers and the right to call his triumph with them, which is blood-brotherhood; perhaps sometimes an exhausted Icelander falls out of the sky, and marries a Harris boy, but grows restless when her relatives fly north in spring. Would they follow her people then, or would we see a new goose family settled on Sleicham or Gumersham?

Chapter 11

Scarista Bird Table

For years, we didn't attempt to feed the garden birds in the winter, on the grounds that food would simply attract the flourishing local tribes of crows, feral cats, rats, blackbacks, and quite likely hyaenas and vultures within our garden walls, thereby threatening the little birds with being made a meal of rather than enjoying a free meal. But there came a day when we were faced with a visitor so lacking in independence that we could no longer harden our hearts. We went out one May morning to find a stray racing pigeon perched on the drawing room windowsill. We had had another such visitor a few years before: that one had flown in through the open window, and was discovered roosting beside the posy on the mantelpiece, looking distinctly rococo. That first pigeon pecked alongside the hens for a fortnight and departed refreshed, leaving the windowsill mounded with pigeon manure. But our new visitor was less brash. He sidled winningly up to the hens and they pecked him; he waddled disconsolately away, and Shep rounded him up. He hunched dizzily in the centre of the roundup till rescued by human hands. Percy, as Sarah and her friends of course named him, lacked drive. We transferred him to the herb garden, which is theoretically out of bounds to hens, and not big enough for a really satisfactory roundup. There he perched picturesquely on the low stone wall, or occasionally on the sun-warmed slates above, sheltering under the carved stone bench when it rained. He ate a prodigious amount of grain from the children's hands, and cooed amorously at everyone and everything. He was very decorative, and totally out of place; we have a few shy slender rock doves on our coasts, but nothing of the trusting eye, rainbow iridescence and sleek rotundity which characterised Percy. Sarah was delighted with this exotic pet, and fed him more and more grain till his corporation fairly billowed. Even Percy couldn't eat quite all of it, and the beds and paths of the herb garden began to sprout green corn shoots. After a couple of months, he began to fly further afield, and one day returned with one of those same wild rock doves. He murmured and cooed and ruffled to her on the roof, but she seemed unimpressed. Though she seemed to

125

concede that he was a good provider: we hoped for a match when we saw her packing away grain under Percy's indulgent eye. Then one day, there were no pigeons. The children concluded that Penelope had beguiled him away to join her wild friends, and still look for them in any flock we see, but the truth was probably less romantic: on the very day that Percy disappeared, I had noticed a couple of harassed peregrines with a ravenous newly-fledged youngster quartering the neighbourhood. As a conservationist, one should of course make peregrines welcome, but I grudged them that meal.

Bereft of her feathered pet, Sarah began to make noises about a bird table. She had a copy of a Young Ornithologist's Club magazine, with a colourful picture of tits and finches queuing up at a suburban bird table. 'You won't get any of these here, you know,' we told her, and 'Not till October, anyway.' This latter on the grounds that it's bad for birds to feed them unsuitable titbits during the breeding season, and our starlings were plainly still breeding: third time that year, in spite of pinching Percy's unsuitable corn. More to the point was that by October we would have got rid of the guests; for Percy's corn had also attracted a pretty young female rat, who now lived in the wall just outside the dining room window. She was innocently tame, not at all put off by onlookers. She embarrassed Andrew and our staff hugely. They hoped she would go away when the corn supply failed. In fact, she left discreetly when Morag, much provoked, threatened with Gaelic imprecations to take a broomstick to her.

Come October, a makeshift bird table was duly installed in an angle of the walls to discourage herring gulls, which dislike landing in confined spaces. It turned out that the main attraction of a bird table from Sarah's point of view was the bird pudding which was apparently *de rigueur* to lay on it. The children spent a greasy evening melting vast quantities of fat and stirring in bagfuls of oatmeal, lentils, raisins, sunflower seeds, muesli, peanuts – you name it, it was crunched all over the kitchen floor and smeared on the chairs. The impressive-sized roasting tin full of Bird Pudding was rationed out for a week, by the end of which time Sarah had lost interest in bird tables; but by then, thirty or so starlings were waiting hopefully each morning, so feeding had to continue. As predicted, not a single bluetit or greenfinch, not a crossbill or goldcrest, has come to the feast. On a good day, we get forty or fifty starlings, almost as many sparrows, a couple of herring gulls, a hoody crow or so, and perhaps a wren tidying up once the party is over. One of the more independent-spirited hens has decided it's worth risking an apoplexy flying over the gate to attend such a feast, and remaining afterwards to scratch up the plants. Herring gulls, we have learned, soon become tame enough to land in confined spaces with nonchalant ease. When we omit to put out food for them, they perch in the carpark on top of the guests' cars, making horrible threatening noises. The trails of muddy footprints and squirts of corrosive guano they leave on the Mercedes and BMWs are almost as embarrassing as the rat in the wall. They have other tricks, too. One day we were startled to see two of our girls rushing through the garden from the annexe building at the back, leaping the fence, and charging blindly into the field. Was the place on fire? Had Mr Room 7 attempted rape? Not at all: a herring gull was the culprit. The annexe bedrooms are in a single-storey building, and when the girls clean in the morning, they put the stainless steel milk jugs from the tea-trays out on the doorstep so that Shep can drink the leftover milk. (If this sounds eccentric, it is fairly typical of the establishment.) An envious herring gull had snatched up one of the jugs and made off with it, dropping it several times from a height to smash it open, by analogy with sea urchins and other hard-shelled food. Having failed to extract anything edible, the thief retired to the chimney stack, swearing.

The bold scavenging behaviour of gulls had always made us think that they would be all too easy to tame, should we end up with an injured one on our hands. This autumn, we had a chance to learn wisdom, when we came across a juvenile herring gull with a dragging wing running along the road. Injured birds are often surprisingly difficult to catch, but this one was easy – it tripped over its damaged wing and lay squawking with its feet in the air. I grabbed it, meaning only to wring its neck to save it a lingering end, but Andrew noticed how bright and lively its eyes looked, and since we thought we knew herring gulls are bold spirits and will eat anything, we decided to take it home. We have about an acre of ground, and as long as the bird would come for food, as surely any gull would, it could have the run of the place and roost with the hens. The wing had obviously been broken at the shoulder for days: it hung only by a thread of skin, and there were maggots in the wound. We amputated it, applied wound dressing powder, and offered the patient salmon roes and liver. It gulped these voraciously from our hands, then scuttled to cover under a bush in the front garden. This seemed fairly promising. Our new pet was assumed to be a 'he' and christened Sammy by the children, and installed in a temporary pen under the kitchen window, where there is a small shed near the house wall, leaving a gap to creep into for shelter and privacy.

Next day looked less hopeful. Sammy wouldn't eat, didn't preen, and hunched in the rain looking damp, bedraggled and wretched. We caught him again to sort out the remaining maggots with paraffin, and he screeched in open-beaked terror. We expected him to die and rather wished he would, as the difficulties of protecting a one-winged gull not tame enough to handle were beginning to present themselves. However, by the following day, he pecked at some of the fish we threw to him, and looked a little less bedraggled. That evening, we saw him preening, and realised from this that he did not intend to give up the ghost; but it taxed us to know what to do to improve his lot. Within a week he would come out of his hidey-hole behind the shed at a repeated call of 'Sammy-Sammy-Sammy' and at first we thought this very hopeful. We imagined him hopping onto our knees, and following us round the yard, as the hens do. In fact, he had reached his limit: he would run eagerly almost within arm's length, then stop, hesitate, hurl himself sideways and try to force his way out through the wire netting. The first few times there was a genuine conflict: he would have liked to come nearer, but after an internal struggle, the urge to flee took over. Soon and the few seconds of hesitation disappeared: each time he was called or offered food, he would come confidently to his predetermined boundary, then immediately sidestep, and rush to and fro at the netting. After an adequate escape bid, he would subside, seemingly satisfied, and betake himself calmly enough to preening, eating or bathing in his washing-up bowl. He didn't seem unhappy, but his ritualised escape movements were uncomfortably reminiscent of caged zoo animals pacing up and down. Besides, it was an indignity to him to be stared at through the wire mesh. The hens came down from their quarters at the back to give their opinion, and it was derogatory. 'Nasty deformed thing, where's its other wing?' 'Why's it getting fish? We only get mash and vegetable peelings!' 'Never laid an egg in its life! Disgraceful!' 'Peck it and see what it does.' The prisoner's treatment from the other residents was ignominious, too. Jet plodded up and down frowning in front of the wire, in his best prison warder manner, occasionally sniffing the air in a rather fee-fi-fo sort of way, which made poor Sammy nervous. Shep and Roy, our canine neighbours, leapt the wire and stole his fish, causing him to scuttle behind the shed. As for Erica, she tramped all over his pen during her raids on the hens' mash bin, which also stood by the kitchen window, and drank his bath dry.

After a fortnight of such indignities, we tried Sammy with freedom. He was relaxed enough in the yard, but as soon as he turned the corner and saw the sea, he shot off down the drive, over the cattle grid, and along the road. Immediately, clamouring gulls descended on him, knocking him off his feet. We rushed to the rescue and sadly carried him home, feeling guilty about his un-wrung neck; but it's one thing killing a bird which is in dire straits, another doing away with one which is perfectly healthy and has become a children's pet.

The three-quarters of Sammy's physique still extant were glow-ingly healthy, his plumage sleek and well groomed, his crop full, his peck forceful and his eyes bright, and he was eating well; though we had discovered that, given the choice, herring gulls are fastidious feeders. Sammy *is* given the choice, as we feel responsible for his maimed condition. We find he will eat fish if very fresh, filleted and cut into fine strips – no coarse lumps or yesterday's leavings, please! – and plaice rather than whiting. After a day or so of fish, he likes to ring the changes with shredded raw liver, grated cheese, or selected lengths of rabbit guts, from the stomach end. His favourite food (but no more than three days on the trot, he gets tired of it) is steak mince.

When the last of the summer guests has gone, we move ourselves and our scruffy belongings into the library, having first moved the cleaner, smarter furnishings out. This year Sammy moved too, to have the run of the front garden, which is safely bounded by a stone wall. With the window between us, we have become quite sociable together. A couple of planks makes a walkway up to the windowsill. Sammy can flip-flop up it on his flat pink feet and watch us curiously as we sit writing or eating inside. He recognises the sound of cutlery and the motion of lifting a mug, and if he likes the look of what we are eating, he sometimes taps on the window for his share. He has his red plastic bath and two rocks to perch on under the window (on the front path in fact: with that and the planks the front door has become inaccessible). We waste many hours enjoying the spectacle of Sammy bathing. His baths are highly expressive: they usually take place when he feels he has done rather well, after he has caught a worm, or when he has seen off the two-winged herring gull which sometimes swoops in to steal his dinner. He stands in the basin, tossing water vigorously over his head and shoulders, ruffling up his feathers and shaking them out again with brisk it's-good-to-be-alive movements, so that we don't feel so bad about not wringing his neck. With the open space of the lawn, the gravel paths, and the impressive thirty-foot cliff of the house, he now enjoys a fairly natural habitat, which he seems to appreciate. He is, if anything, less willing to approach humans closely than before, but far more relaxed as long as we keep a yard or so away. Through the window we can watch him in his beautiful bird-sleep, with his beak tucked under his lovely white-edged buff feathers and his eyes gradually closing. He seems particularly soothed by strains of Mozart from within.

Birds are often aesthetic creatures. We noticed after a week or so that it was not the wind, but Sammy, which had collected interesting pebbles, sticks and an old oyster shell at the edge of the grass near his bath. Sarah and her friends were despatched to the beach forthwith, and returned with more shells, a seaweed holdfast on a pebble, a crab claw and suchlike, adding new items from time to time. Sammy takes passing fancies to this or that: his longest standing treasure is one of those small oval floats, stuck with a few barnacles. He peers solemnly through first one end and then the other, pecks it, and carries it from place to place with a rapacious air. Presumably he is using the movements a wild adult gull would make when sizing up a large potentially edible object. I doubt if he knows what he is looking for, since he stands aside in dismay from actually edible substances if they are more than worm-sized. I suspect that if he had a real sea-urchin or oyster presented to him, he would wait for it to be opened and chopped into bite-sized pieces; perhaps he wasn't weaned when we got him, or whatever the bird equivalent is. I used to think his one-winged state made him incapable of balancing well enough to tug at large pieces of food, but judging by the verve with which he attacks and carries his float, this is not so. His favourite toys, particularly the float, are gathered close to his bath. This area seems to be definitely his territory; he will repel other birds from it angrily, and if Jet comes into the garden, Sammy stands possessively in his patch until the evil Monster is actually hoovering up his mince or drinking his bath. It surprised us to realise that a gull outside the breeding season, and a juvenile at that, has a home base which feels comfortable and worth defending; and it is even more astonishing that poor earthbound juvenile Sammy is sufficiently imbued with territorial authority to drive a healthy adult herring gull away. Doubtless, to a gull, the size of Sammy's cliff, the whiteness of his pebble 'beach', and the ample supply of good food he attracts so effortlessly all inspire respect.

The starlings, though, are anything but respectful. Sammy squawks at them angrily when they nip in and steal his rations, but they are much too quick and cheeky for him. His main defensive manoeuvre is to stand in front of his food, facing the enemy, but the enemy simply hops in under his tail and grabs the booty. After they have stolen it all, they line up on the wall and mock him with herring gull calls: they make these a lot more realistically than Sammy, whose voice has not broken yet. Feeding Sammy has become something of a battle of wits, and the starlings' wits are usually quicker than ours. Fortunately, gulls feed readily late in the day, when starlings have all flown off in a riotous body to their sociable roosts, so at least he can have supper unmolested. In fact, Sammy is altogether pretty much of a problem. He rarely looks nowadays as if he would prefer to have had his neck wrung, but he does seem very attached to his home outside the front door.

When the guests return next summer, they may well be puzzled, or even aggrieved, to find that they have to wade through a basin of water, clamber over several rocks, and duck under some planks to reach the front door.

Sammy isn't the only problem on our hands. As time goes on and more and more birds and animals hang around our premises in expectation of food, making sure they all get their rations and don't filch anyone else's becomes increasingly difficult. This year we have attempted some rationalisation, by feeding them all in different areas: the hens in the henhouse, Sammy in the front garden, Erica in the carpark, the garden birds in the herb garden, the wild gulls in the field, Jet in the kitchen, and Shep and Roy (who appear most mornings with shameless lies about starvation at home) in the back porch. The new system might work if we had seven people to feed them all simultaneously. As it is, the three of us rush around for half an hour each morning with an increasing sensation of everything getting out of control. Erica bolts her pony nuts and craftily appears at the henhouse door, offering to kick anyone who attempts to carry the hen's bucket past her greedy nose. The starlings are driven off their crumbs by the gulls, and swoop round to steal Sammy's shredded fish. Shep and Roy have jumped the fence and are devouring the gulls' kipper skins. Poor old crippled Jet has been abandoned in the kitchen while we all dash around standing guard over this one and that one, and now lies howling in an exaggerated manner so that he has to have a second breakfast in compensation. Thereafter he goes out and spitefully devours a very old sheep's neck that Roy has buried in the daffodils for future use. Meanwhile Sammy hovers around him looking for pickings, while the starlings steal his mince behind his back, and Erica has opened the shed door with her nose and got into the hens' grain bin, and the children have found a really lovely rat in the humane trap, and they've given it some grain, and couldn't we keep it as a pet? and by the way, do I know the wee mouse in the attic is back, and they've put down sunflower seeds for him?

For some years we have had the unrealised ambition of acquiring land as a nature reserve, but our present *ménage* is more like a badly run zoo. Still, it quite pleased me the other day to see ten rabbits, one rat and twenty sparrows confidently approaching for their share when I threw down the hens' corn. The rabbit shall lie down with the rat and a little hen shall lead them.

Chapter 12

November's Lambs

It was a magical morning. The sky arched as smooth and blue as a starling's egg, the water answering the colour perfectly, except in the boat's shadow, where was steep green depth. The outlines of land were sharp, the tints soft and changing in the pellucid air with its hints of rainbows: a teasing oscillation between clarity and uncertainty, which is the soul of this wild place. It was November, but hopeful, springlike. There may be one or two such days in a dim, dismal month of blustery wind and rough sea. We had waited three autumns for a day like this, to be sure of good enough weather to suit our time limit. We were at the outside of our restricted sailing range, though it had been motoring, not sailing, all the way: enough wind to make sailing possible in the time at our disposal would almost certainly have created too heavy a swell to allow landing. With the engine cut after an hour and a half of chugging, the silence was not so much absence of noise, as a labyrinth of quiet sounds: the slop and trickle of water rising and falling on the weed-covered rocky arms of the bay, the whisper and hiss on the sandy beach, the muffled boom of the Atlantic in the caves and fissures of the farther side; and mingled with the sea noises, the voices of the people we had come to visit. This is a grey seal island. We could hear them before we saw them; then as we neared the bay, scattered boulders turned into big bull seals, raising heads, shuffling a few uneasy paces. The brown and tawny hillside above moved here and there, resolving into seal bodies, asleep or half awake, and the white blobs were not sheep, but seal pups. We began to exclaim and point; heads turned on land, heads rose out of the water, with eyes expressive of reproach, and the voices were reproachful too: really they would much rather we hadn't come. We felt like Balmoral tourists trying to spy on the royal family, climbing uncivilly on fences and peering through treetops. We lowered our voices, abashed. We must be on our best behaviour.

We had been told many times that seal breeding grounds are squalid, smelly places, overcrowded and littered with dead and sickly pups; that the adults bicker for room, mow down each other's offspring, and head for the sea deserting the pups at the first sign of trouble. We glided silently in, under sail now, waiting for it all to start, for a great wave of bodies caterpillaring down the beach, or worse, heading uphill towards the top of the western cliffs. We had heard how on one occasion many seals had thrown themselves a hundred feet down these terrible precipices into the sea. But the men who saw that had gone to shoot moulted seal pups, and arrived, no doubt, with the noise and swagger guilty humans use to glamourise bad actions in their own eyes. We would have turned without landing if such a panic had started, but there was little sign of it as we approached the beach. Some of the nearer cows lolloped down the sand and cruised round us in the shallows; some of the further ones humped nearer to their pups; some of the most distant, well up the hillside, woke up and went back to sleep. A couple of very young pups on the sand shuffled nearer to us, hopeful of a feed from these large moving objects. We anchored with as little fuss as possible. Paying the rope out, I saw a head submerge, followed by the porpoise roll of a sleek back, as the nearest seal dived to investigate the hook and chain on the sandy bottom.

We were being watched: with curiosity by the swimming seals, who couldn't resist a closer and a closer look, being safe in their own element; with hope by the two little pups and by a few more among the rounded boulders of the upper beach, though most of that company were asleep, draped over the stones in total relaxation; with drowsy half-interest by the two nearest territorial bulls, nodding off in the blissful sunshine; with anxiety by a mother seal suckling a young pup on an intertidal rock very near us. Beyond the beach, heads were raised in mild unease, voices quavered reproach, soft eyes questioned us. No one charged at us angrily, no one snapped at our ankles, no one threw his considerable weight about. The smallest adult grey seal is heavier than a big man, with teeth larger than the largest dog's; and like large dogs, they use them mainly for eating, otherwise with restraint. As we were not competing for mates or food, and were not fish, we would not be harmed.

We breasted the rise at the top of the beach, preparing ourselves for squalor, and saw pure pastoral. On the gentle grass slope between the sheltered bay where we had landed and the cliff-bound western shore, several hundred seals lay at ease in the sun, basking as only those who spend most of their lives in cold water know how: great Roman-nosed bulls, smaller sweet-faced cows, plump little moulters, white bleating sucklers. Neptune leaning shepherd-like on his trident would not have been unexpected in the midst of this flock. When missionaries evangelised the Innuit, they found no lambs and substituted the word for seal pup to express the concept of the Lamb of God. If the Innuit had known and hunted only warthogs or hippopotami, the missionaries might have had to make do with a less graceful approximation; nevertheless, the chance equivalent is poignant. Seal pups of all species at the whitecoat stage are the picture of vulnerable innocence. They cry 'Mam', their huge dark eyes weep tears when things go wrong. This is the truth and pseudo-scientific disclaimers are evasions: the cry, like a human infant's prelinguistic 'Mama', is for food and comfort; their tears flow more easily than ours because they have no tear-ducts, but their reasons for weeping are the same, hunger, fear, discomfort, perplexity.

The very youngest felt none of these and approached trustingly, being just old enough to realise that large things which move might provide milk. They were still thin inside their folds of loose skin, with over-large heads and foreflippers. Their creamy natal coat lasts for the fortnight of suckling, and during that time they plump up enormously on the mother's rich milk, increasing from a birth weight of about thirty-two pounds to over a hundred; it is reckoned that a pup below ninety pounds at weaning has little chance of surviving through its first winter. We found many little hundred-pound barrels, asleep with tight bellies uppermost and flippers spread wide, showing the bare palms. After they are a day or so old, the whitecoats begin to be worldly wise, and no longer shuffle up to strangers. Those who were awake goggled at us mildly as long as we kept two or three yards distance, but at a nearer approach, they would snarl and weep, and back away ineffectively, much too fat to escape if we had intended human harm, but fast enough to get out of the way of strange adult seals, except during heated territorial arguments.

Disturbance to nursing mother seals, either directly or by causing general alarm, can be fatal to the pups, who have to put on such an enormous amount of blubber to withstand their first winter, and handling of pups is particularly inadvisable, as human scent may confuse the mother and cause her to reject her infant; so we kept on the move, and to the outer edge of the colony between the sea and the hillside, where the seals were most thinly spread. Some of the cows there had left for the water, but those remaining, though far shyer than the pups, tolerated us as long as we kept about thirty yards away and moved slowly. I was surprised how little our scent seemed to bother them at this distance; perhaps as they were so well dispersed on this less populous area they did not communicate fear to each other. A few left in a great hurry, but the others, with plenty of space between them and no barrier of seal bodies blocking escape, did not panic. We avoided the more crowded central ground, but could see from above that it was thick with seals: that area was obviously favoured for its string of muddy ponds, delightful wallows for seals of all ages, and practice swimming pools for the moulted pups. This oozy playground gives easy access by the sand beach to the sea; seals from the fringes of the colony had a much more laborious hump over grass and rocks. Yet it has been found on at least one other seal island, North Rona, that seals which pup well inland spend more time with their babies, and offer them greater protection against the clumsy passage of other seals, particularly the heavy bulls; and that in the very crowded areas, it becomes difficult for the mother to suckle her pup because of the constant disturbance of other seals going to and fro, and bickering over territory. The mother regards as 'territory' a certain-sized space round her pup, which she marks out by shuffling round it soon after birth. If the pup moves, it carries this space with it, in the mother's eyes, and she will beat even a large bull out of the charmed circle.

There were few arguments in progress on that kindly November day. Here and there a louder and more querulous voice was raised above the usual quiet wavering plaints of the female seals; here and there a bull roused himself and raised an impressive head to inspect a rival who had shuffled in his direction; but on the whole, the bulls seemed too engrossed in sleep and sunshine to bother with much else. They would permit a closer approach than the cows. Having peered to ascertain that we were too weedy to be rivals and too ugly to be wives, they dropped heads and went back to sleep: they snore wonderfully. Andrew met one at close quarters on the beach. Looking down on the confrontation, I was slightly alarmed. The seal seemed elderly, tired and thin, but he was some eight feet long with a head the size of a steer's, and moved with astonishing speed. Andrew felt flattered to be worth his attention, till he realised that the old fellow was not contesting with him, but escaping from a more vigorous-looking bull who had just come ashore and flumped proprietorially to where the older seal had been basking on the sand. The fleeing animal might have been an old non-territorial bull, or a territory holder who had been deposed or had simply given up exhausted late in the season: there is often some takeover of territory as time goes on, for the bulls adopt these stances from early September onwards, and survive sparring with rivals and frequent mating on no food and very little sleep; hence the doziness and slack skins of the males we saw that day, with just two or three weeks of the season to go.

The mating arrangements of the grey seal used to be regarded as a harem system, with a lordly bull attracting and guarding a bevy of submissive cows. Fashions in seeing have changed in a feminist age, among laymen and scientists alike – what price objectivity? There is none! We are no more free of bias today than the most patriarchal Victorian, so that to a modern observer it seems apparent that the cows call the tune: they go where they wish, subject only to bickering with other cows over pup-space. If charged by an angry bull, all they need do is turn on one side and vibrate a flipper, and he will back off sheepishly. A female can shoo a bull away even from the centre of his own territory, if he is too near her infant. The bull's territories are defined only with reference to other males, who will contest fiercely until boundaries are decided. A male scoops up any female who cares to come in and see his etchings, but she may wander away when she feels like it: he may occasionally pursue a retreating cow, but he daren't leave his territory unguarded for long, and will not necessarily keep her where he wants her. She comes ashore to where her pup is, not to a particular bull; bulls come to land to beget, cows to give birth. A female will not mate until she is ready, usually about the time of weaning, and the bull who tries anything on too soon is likely to get bitten for his cheek. It has been estimated from growth rings in the cement layer of their teeth that females often live to be over thirty, males seldom as much as twenty. Few males hold territories for more than three or four years; though they are sexually mature at five or six, they are not physically massive enough to impress other bulls till the age of nine or ten. The young bulls and virgin cows probably have their youthful fling in the waters near the breeding grounds, but no one has ascertained this, as mating usually takes place in the water, where individuals are hard to identify.

Holding territory is an onerous task, which is why not all bulls stay the course, but are replaced by others near the end of the season. The bulls may stay put for up to three months, entering the water only to mate or to pursue rivals. They don't leave even to feed, living entirely off their reserves of blubber. During this time, several relays of cows come and go, hauling out a little before giving birth, nursing their pups for a fortnight, mating and taking to the sea again. By the end of the lactation period, the cows too have lost condition, as they feed little or not at all during this shore-based part of their year, so that all the seventy-pound weight gain of a fat pup comes directly from the mother's blubber. They leave the breeding areas inseminated, but in no fit physical state to start another pregnancy. They are helped by the phenomenon of delayed implantation: it is not until after about three and a half months, during which they feed voraciously and moult, that the fertilised ovum adheres to the uterine wall and begins to develop.

What of the abandoned infants? At two weeks old, they are almost spherical, having filled – and stretched – every wrinkle in the loose skin they were born with. When suckling stops, they immediately moult their white baby fur, showing the pretty silvery grey spotted skin which has brought many of them to the flenser's knife, but which if allowed to remain on its owner's portly form will last it for the next fifteen months or so. The sudden abandonment of the pups seems like a cruel fate, but in fact after a few relatively immobile days brought about by excessive obesity – the pup may be too fat for its flippers to reach the ground with sufficient purchase – the moulters begin to investigate their surroundings, swimming and splashing in the wallows and in sheltered rock pools, sometimes chasing pieces of plastic flotsam or birds, or just dozing in the water. At first, they are too buoyant to dive: once sufficiently slimmed by their enforced fast, they leave for the sea, where they must learn to find food unaided, though watching the techniques of older seals may well be within their capabilities. However that may be, the time following is very hazardous for them. Many are carried far away by winds and surface currents, and end up stranded, dead or alive, on other coasts. Others simply fail to fish expertly enough to maintain body weight, and die of cold in their first winter. Maintenance, not gain, is the best they can do, and few yearling seals weigh as much as a newly weaned pup: that is why it is so vital for them to be fattened to absurd proportions before the mother leaves.

But this gaunt future of which they know nothing casts no shadow for the young moulters. They are cheerful, placid creatures. As we came down the hill, five or six of them were playing in the limpid rock pools, bobbing and porpoising in the incoming tide, floating back up or belly up, watching us with friendly eyes. Grey seals are often described as unsociable, but these young ones were clearly companions, playing an endless, indolent follow-my-leader, out of the blue pool into the green shallows of the bay, all heads up, all heads down, back to the pool: no horseplay, but play nevertheless, between the blissful elements of cool, stroking, tickling water and warm sunny air.

We left them with regret. I think they were sorry, too; they were too young to know any better. Moulters of previous years could not pass on a warning after they had become trinkets for tourists. Perhaps they would not even have had the concept of *enemy* to make a warning out of. Does a creature which looks with such friendly curious eyes connect a blow or a shot with its agent? The nervous cow at the tideline rocks still lay nursing her young pup. She moaned, with weeping eyes; she was afraid, a dim awareness that something was not right, that the protective snarl and whirring flipper which would send off a quarter-ton male of her own species, with his wolf's teeth and grizzly bear paws, would not always elicit chivalry.

We looked back across the wallows, at all the lovely curves and ellipses of resting seals, creatures without angles or straight lines.

A few heads were raised again in unease, soft eyes still questioned us; their question could not be framed to fit the terrible human answer. They know our species cannot want their wives or a space to put a pup, that we don't eat seals, or we would set on them with famished teeth. What, then? How?

Seals cannot know about the salmon farmers' quick buck, or about souvenirs for tourists; about cure-all oil invested with semi-magical properties; about the Popish Vulgar eating seals in Lent; about the Vulgar of the other denomination, too fine and dainty to taint their fingers with smelly seal flesh, conveying it to their mouths 'with a long pointed stick instead of a Fork.' Century after century of crazy answers could not be fitted to the sane question.

Why do we continue to harry them? They eat too much; they spread codworm, which spoils the look of marketable fish; they erode vegetation on offshore islands; they are overcrowded, it's for their own good; they take salmon – sportsmen's salmon, netsmen's salmon, poachers' salmon, fish farmers' salmon.

'The Liver of a Seal being dry'd and pulverizd, and afterwards a little of it drunk 'with Milk, Aquavitae or red Wine, is good against the Fluxes.' What good reason have we? We are not starving for want of fish. More than half of what we catch is turned into fertilisers and animal feed anyway. Besides, most of what seals catch is small uncommercial stuff from the sea bottom: they are too slow to catch such fine prey as salmon, unless it is kept conveniently caged or netted while they seize it. Again, seal numbers are constrained by the availability of suitable breeding sites: those left to them after the spread of human population are few and unfavourable; no fear of their numbers exploding, as ours do.

Official culls come and go. Since 1976, no licences have been issued to 'take' grey seals on the breeding grounds, but fishermen are still entitled to kill any seals showing interest in their work. Yet the lobbying is kept up, a senseless, spiteful whine for more culling, for the official stamp of respectability on the nasty deed. At any time, government might yield to the pressure for reasons of political convenience. Then the moulters might again look curiously at the rifles; or perhaps a total wipeout of whole colonies from helicopters, 'more humane' say some parties. Canadian wolves know whether or not that method is humane: it is certainly lucrative to helicopter hire companies, and lovely fun for marks-men.

Meanwhile, new reasons are found to kill seals. I heard of fifteen shot in one day in a small area of Lewis. Their crime was loitering round a fish farm. Fish farmers don't kill seals – they 'control predators'. They don't kill only seals, they kill otters, eider duck, herons, shags, cormorants and mergansers as well. That is the price paid for the artificially coloured, inhumanely reared, drug-laden hunk of 'Scottish Salmon' on the fishmonger's slab. It is an un-wholesome meal for any thinking person, and a crazy answer.

'Some of the Natives wear a Girdle of Seal-Skin about the Middle, for removing the Sciatica, as those of the Shire of *Aberdeen* wear it to remove the Chin-Cough.'

Much good may it do them.

Chapter 13

Black Winter

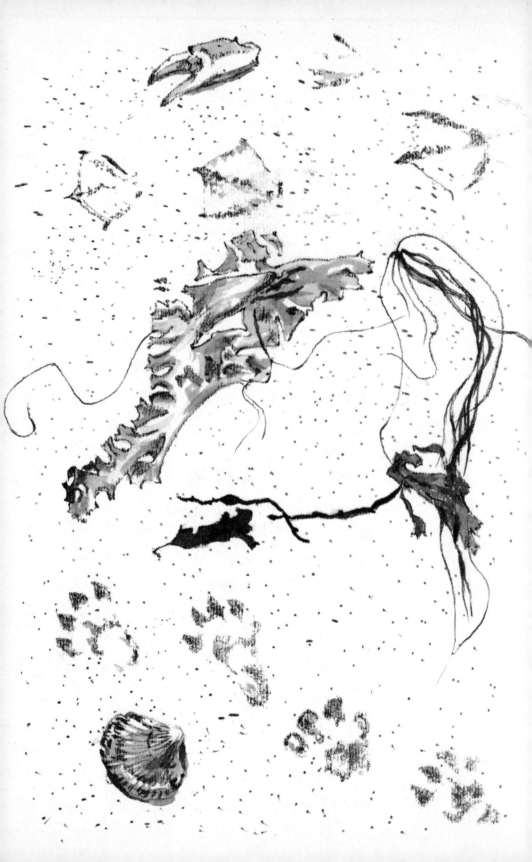

In a country with no leaves to fall, the signs of winter are read in the weather and rapidly shortening daylight. In Gaelic tradition, winter begins at Hallowe'en: a meaningful division. Though October is often wild and stormy, sunrise and sunset still contain some semblance of a day; but November brings dark mornings and dark evenings, with the sun's arc in the sky decreasing till it is scarcely significant. The waterlogged fields may be touched sometimes with slanting golden light, the clouds suffused with rose and lemon at the ends of the day, but the sun is losing potency, seems scarcely a force to be reckoned with, sliding downhill towards the dark solstice.

A Hebridean winter is in two halves, black and white. The slowed-down darkening months of November and December, with rain and mist, gales bringing more rain, endless nights; the vigorous freezing months of January and February, with frost and snow, lustier gales that scour the sky blue, hopes of light and spring. 'Gaoth bhog nan duldachd, gaoth fhuar nan faoilteach', a Gaelic proverb has it: the soft wind of dark winter, the cold wind of hoary winter.

November sometimes begins with a period of still weather, 'feath nan eun', the calm of the birds, a time when it was said even the birds were mute. There is some truth in the old belief. Benign weather at that time of year sees the birds feeding as fast as possible, without time to utter. Such a calm for us is positively the last chance of sailing for the year. Not that winter is an unmitigated succession of gales; but they are certainly too frequent and too fierce to risk leaving the boat on a mooring. The cold becomes a problem, too, or at least more of a problem, though it is nearly always cold on the water even in summer. Once the sea temperature drops to 8° or 9°C it is difficult to keep up body heat, even wearing so many layers of patent sailing clothing that it becomes a major effort to bend or stretch, or even to breathe, since manufacturers of foul-weather gear seem to specialise in zips which garrotte the wearer. Some hardy fishermen continue to go out in winter when the weather is passable, apparently dressed only in boiler-suits and oilskins, and how they survive I don't know; but by November most of the small craft are up from the water, and the coloured floats of the moorings have a deserted air, like an out-of-season promenade at a seaside resort, with stacked-up chairs in shuttered cafés, and waiting gulls.

The waiting gulls hang about at Leverburgh harbour too, but to better effect: November is sheep-slaughtering time, and much offal is dumped in the sea, to the great joy of the blackbacks. The sheep's owners enjoy a feast as well; this is the traditional time for fresh home-grown meat, better than anything out of the shops, and joints are eaten convivially at home and given generously as gifts, with some to salt for those that like it that way, and plenty over to put in the freezer. Even the scurviest sheepdog has good Martinmas bones to gnaw. Only the sheep are dismal about it.

But back to the last sail of this year. A day of unsurpassable beauty, with opal colours on all the islands, violet shading into rose and pink into apricot and gold, all in a sea of pale enamelled blue: the tints of sunrise or sunset at noon. The low sunlight tensed the day, reminding of long darkness close at hand. We could have gone to far-out Pabbay or Shillay – had taken extra petrol to that end, in case the wind dropped; but somehow we made excuses, and agreed that the actually abnormally small swell on Irishman's Rock looked as if it might get up. The cold seeping inexorably through all the layers of polar this and thermal that was ominous. The calm of the birds made things unusually quiet. Only a few black guillemots in winter plumage bobbed around us. Suddenly, we found ourselves goggling in frozen horror at a ground-down molar of a rock, hissing quietly under the beginnings of surf. 'Not where I thought it was,' said Andrew. Marked on the chart, dries three metres, Bomasanhui: a sort of South-Pacific-cannibal-looking name. We stopped pretending we might go to Pabbay, and turned tail. Cold numbs judgment as well as flesh, and it is disconcerting to find you have been bearing down on a perfectly visible reef for several minutes without reacting. Still it was sad to stow the sails for the last time, and to bring the boat in to the pier for trailing home. The islands and landmarks of summer glowed in the low light: red beacon on Sgeir Volinish, black beacon on Red Rock, Dubh Sgeir beacon in a black and orange football jersey, Jane's

Tower in green and white, gateways to so many little worlds: Stromay beset by whirlpools, Saghay Bheag with celandines bigger than buttercups, Suem of the terns and tiny beach, lush Sleicham, sealy Langasker; Ensay which the children love, Killegray where the skuas teased us; Langay, long island; Gilsay, sheer island; Groay, gravel island; Scaravay, cormorant island; Dunaarin, the sentinel. For half the year they are more familiar than our four walls at home.

Now the dark part of the year closes in. Bonfire night, with many bonfires. Guy Fawkes was a Catholic, crime enough, but the Presbyterian children burn him without malice: they just love bonfires. Hebrideans all do: the men burning byre-litter in March are as cheerful as the November children, moor-burning is carried out with devastating abandon, our local tramp dances round the rubbish tip when it is lit on Saturday afternoons. One needn't look for relics of Celtic fire-worship: the climate is enough reason. To put it another way, perhaps the Celtic ancestors felt the same way. Their vision of Hell, like the Norsemen's Niflheim, was a chilly region of ice and freezing fog. Fire was, and is, the precious element of domestic and convivial comfort. 'Come in to the fire!' is the immediate welcome to a caller, for whose pleasure the hearth will be stacked high with peats, which smoke with the fragrance of summer heather. Peat reek scents the air of every Hebridean village, as much a feature of the modern picture-windowed crofthouse as of the black house of the past. The tradition of the welcoming fireside, indicative of peace and plenty, is given added meaning by the lengthy careful labour devoted to laying in the peat, cutting, drying, stacking and carrying home. It was, and still is, a sort of harvest. There's no prospect of a poor man leaving the gathering of winter fu-el till the Feast of Stephen in this part of the world; nowadays the Social will buy him coal, but in the past no peats meant no fire – no cooking, no drying, no warmth, no home, for the thatches of the black houses disintegrated rapidly, once damp. The St Kildans had no easily accessible peat, and burned turf instead, a slow, smouldering, reluctant fire. In the moist salt-laden air, their clothes can never have been dry; their domestic arrangements sound extraordinarily dreary.

'Just sitting in by the fire' is a positive feature of island life in winter, a real, grateful pleasure in the contrast between inside and out. Rain, wind and darkness by night, rain, wind and half-light by day, till the grass looks more dead than natural vegetation should ever look, as if poisoned by darkness, livid and slimy; indistinct horizons between fuming sea and trailing cloud; fat rams chasing scrawny ewes, who seem unenthusiastic – What! And start that all over again?

The rams are the only animals in fine fettle. Most of them are handsome blackface beasts with majestic curly horns, though some Suffolks and Cheviots are used to improve lamb carcase size and twinning prospects. They are brought in from the hill in October and tethered or enclosed for a month on good grazing near the houses, where their masters can keep an indulgent eye on them, feed them with extra titbits, and patiently disentangle them when they tie themselves up in their tethers. For most of the year, rams live in peaceful brotherly bands, apparently with none of the tussling for dominance and sheer rattiness which the ewes show towards each other; but by the time they have been tethered for several weeks in sight of their comrades but not close enough for friendly conversation, the dim brains inside those thick and much-jarred skulls have begun to run on other things. When they have eaten as much as they can stuff, they stop eating and look vacant, and then restless, as if they have just thought of something they meant to remember – what was it? What's that over there? Big ugly thing with horns! Butt it! Oh, sorry, it's you, Hector. And they fall to eating again, till a sudden flicker of something has them straining once more on their tethers, squaring up for battle.

Even when they are finally turned in with the ewes, they don't quite seem able to recollect what it was they meant to remember. If a ewe walks away from a ram who is trying to mount her (as she often does) he may simply stand looking puzzled for some minutes before wandering off to graze. Some contests between rivals are conducted with fire and dash, with the proper ritual movements of parallel walking, broadside threatening, headlong flight of vanquished and head-tossing of victor. But more often, two rams will stand for a whole day phlegmatically butting each other head on at two-minute intervals, without any show of malice. It is the lack of malice that makes rams so dangerous in enclosed spaces: without any preliminary warning such as pawing the ground or lowering the head, a ram may simply butt you, looking all the while as meek, mild and witless as a stained-glass virgin saint, and probably feeling it. Once they start butting, they carry on, if not distracted. There was a nasty case a few years ago of an old lady who had made pets of a neighbour's rams and brought them daily titbits. One day they absent-mindedly butted her to death.

Though the ram's wooing is clumsy, once a ewe has taken to the idea, the pair will nuzzle affectionately before copulating, and graze side by side afterwards; but unlike cows, who seem happiest when rolling their lovely amorous eyes at a resident bull in their midst, the ewes seem to have little time for dalliance. In fact, they have little time for anything except eating, and no wonder, as there is very little to eat. The rams are pampered in preparation for the year's work but the ewes have to take their chance. If a ewe is in poor condition, the worst that can befall the owner is the loss of a lamb: even if the ewe dies, that year's subsidy is still payable on her. But if a ram is not up to scratch, the whole flock may be affected, with many ewes not impregnated for the following year. In summer there is just about enough grazing to keep the ewes fit, if not fat; but in winter it is a pathetic sight to see them grinding away at the worn pasture. Formerly, sheep used to be rigorously excluded from grassland during the early summer, so that the vegetation had a chance to regenerate before winter, but this sensible measure is no longer fully practised. The hill-sheep subsidy, while it has made it economically viable to keep sheep in the exposed highlands and islands, has wrecked land management in this area. Since it is paid per head, there is a strong temptation for the unscrupulous to overstock far beyond the recommended density, and because much of the grazing is common everyone's beasts then suffer. As the land becomes more and more overgrazed, with the attendant problems of erosion and degenerating herbage, it becomes more and more difficult to keep all the sheep (there are an awful lot of them) off the low ground for long enough to allow the vegetation to recover. The subsidy, of course, is intended to pay for supplementary winter feeding; but again, while many owners use it thus to the full, and over, others provide no extra feeding at all. The ewes, all too often, stagger through winter after winter till they eventually collapse and die, light, waterlogged corpses with the bloated bellies of malnutrition. In a way it is not so different from the life of a wild animal, and to that extent far pleasanter than the fate of many modern farm animals: the sheep lead a tranquil enough existence between May and September, though suffering from hunger and cold in winter. However, no wild animal lives at the population density of these sheep, or is obliged to produce young every year – wild goats in similar conditions breed only every other year. Not much wonder the ewes are doubtful about the rams' advances.

Sheep dropping dead is one of the inescapable signs of winter. It is often undergrown first-year animals which succumb first; hoary old ewes persist till the year is coming alive again, and die in the February snow. In this, too, they are like wild animals. The dying, darkening end of the year is inimical to young warm-blooded creatures. I have mentioned already the risks faced by birds and seals in their first winter. Late-reared youngsters are particularly vulnerable: they will not have acquired sufficient body fat before their parents are forced to abandon them and look to their own survival; their hunting skills will not be sufficiently developed before rough weather places additional difficulties in their way; they may even have been separated from parents who were still helping them by early autumn storms. It is sad to find their young skin-and-bone bodies cast up on the tideline, without enough flesh on them even to interest the gulls.

The most pathetic corpse we ever found was not a victim of natural wastage. It was an otter, washed up by the tide in the first cold of November. Two strands of monofilament netting stuck out from the neck. We thought at first the animal had drowned in one of these murderous devices – a bad enough fate for a creature which can hold its breath for four minutes. But the truth was even more horrible. When we turned the body over, we noticed the staring ribs, protruding pelvis and thin fur. On poking at the vile monofilament, we found that it was so deeply embedded that the skin had grown over, but the gullet underneath was constricted. The otter must have swum into the net when it was quite small, bitten itself free, and continued to grow to full size with its throat at baby dimensions, unable to feed or breathe properly. It had died of slow starvation, probably lasting at least six months. Another otter's tracks led up to the corpse and away from it; whether these were a relative's or just a curious visitor's, we don't know, but it was intolerable to see the round pad-prints of the live animal in the sand, next to the poor outspread paws of the dead. Otters use their forepaws like hands, to grasp food and each other, to pat playthings and swipe enemies, to comb their fur and wipe their noses. At that moment I would gladly have used my own hands to strangle any monofilament user.

Lest such feeling over a single animal should seem sentimental, I should point out that vast numbers of mammals and birds are known to die every year as incidental casualties of monofilament nets. The 7000 to 14,000 Dall's porpoises killed annually by the Japanese Pacific squid fishery is a convenient horrifying statistic, but it is not only the Japanese who are guilty, and not only Dall's porpoises which die: all such statistics are almost unbelievably high. The people who use these nets know what they are doing: they haul in the 'incidental' dead.

It is strange how such grisly finds, and the statistics that go with them, are much less easy to forget in this dismal season, when the year itself is slowly dying. A bright summer day is conducive to hope; there is so much beauty prodigally displayed that if not now, then soon, surely, humanity must be persuaded by it to cease to beggar nature; but in the gaunt end of the year any sort of optimism is revealed as so much tinsel.

Whether one's dearest hope is for cosmic improvement or for the local council to mend the potholes in the road, the Hebridean *duldachd* has a way of crushing it. The weather, quite simply, gets people down. The phenomenon is well attested in other northern countries. After a few weeks struggling with slimy ground and rainy wind outside, the perpetual artificial lighting inside (power cuts permitting) bright healthy-mindedness can wear thin. Daylight – real daylight, not half-light – begins to seem like a dream. What it could have been like in the days before artificial light is difficult to imagine. Perhaps people had to work so hard just to survive that they didn't have time for winter *ennui*; it may be an obscene product of material progress, like heart disease and child abuse.

However that may be, lassitude, fatalism and depression affect most people to some extent in winter. The local brand of Presbyterian religion is often blamed by outsiders, and certainly it suits dour winter weather well, with its insistence on predestination, and its psychotic Jehovah subjecting his meek adherents to a sort of LD50 test in temptation. But it can't be the religion that caused the problem in the first place: despite a deep personal contempt for Calvin's God, I still have to kick myself out of bed in the dark mornings. The winter lethargy is just the other side of the coin from the cheerful ceilidhs round a welcoming hearth.

Presbyterianism did, of course, make strenuous efforts to eradicate the pagan festivals which the Catholics had taken over and embellished to cheer up the dreary winter months. The greatest zeal was directed to the celebrations which had already been Christianised, for every staunch Presbyterian loathes popery more than heathenism, since the Pope is Antichrist. Consequently, the unashamedly heathen knees-ups at Hallowe'en and Hogmanay got less of a battering than Martinmas, Candlemas, Christmas or any other sort of mass. But rather than disappearing, all the jollification gravitated in Presbyterian areas towards these pagan observances: Christianity was just left politely out of it, no more incantations to Mary or Bridget or Maelrubha. The churches simply could not squash the winter festivals entirely: they are vital punctuation in a land with a long winter. Who can be sure that the sun will ever grow strong again? By the third week of December, it looks very much like dwindling away. There has to be some festival at the season when it wins and swings higher in the sky again: if not Christmas, then something older than Christmas. Of recent years, since the advent of television, people have tended to celebrate more and more in the same manner as the rest of the country, eating, drinking, visiting, acting Santa to the kids and exchanging Christmas-wrapped presents; though theoretically, at least if ministers and elders are around, they are New Year presents, and the family Christmas tree is kept in a surreptitious corner rather than in the window. But a few older and more mysterious – probably more relevant – customs survive, or are recently defunct: like the Sheep Man who comes visiting with the boys on New Year's Eve, and is chased sunwise round the house by the others with sticks, while they repeat a venerable rhyme, beg gifts of food, and confer blessing on the household. Wonderful material for anthropologists! But anthropologists are awfully serious-minded. To the lads who act out the ancient ritual, it's just a good time, and probably it always was. A laugh and a good time are much better medicine than dim religious rites or wee white pills from the doctor. The sun rises with more confidence after a good evening with your friends.

Chapter 14

White Winter

B ut since the sun has risen again, I can't resist a bit of mysticis-
ing, in spite of my remarks at the end of the previous chapter.
The southern arm of the bay at Scarista is formed by a peninsula
rising out of the low sandy isthmus beyond Northton village. Its
highest point is the rocky summit of Chaipaval, which descends
westward in a long ridge to the remote cliffs of Toe Head and
Liuri. The steep north face of Chaipaval rises from the vast sandy
expanse of Traigh an Taobh Tuath, a hospitable place for birds,
but wild, and not much frequented by people. The south shore of
the peninsula, though, is not wild or remote, or even unfrequented:
in fact, it is one of the most popular summer haunts for tourists
and locals alike, with several pretty sandy beaches accessible from
a real path with possibilities even for pushchairs and grannies, a
very rare thing in Harris. The lower slope of Chaipaval is a wide
sweep of grassland, which in summer is jewelled and scented with
wild flowers, one of the best remaining machair pastures in the
island. This meadow is bounded by a fine drystone wall, made of
stone painstakingly cleared from the area below. Above it the
hillside rises sharply, bare rock interspersed with acid heath. The
startlingly smooth green below the wall is visible at all seasons,
even from a long way out at sea, a friendly smile on the ancient
familiar face of Chaipaval. This little paradise, so loved today by
picnickers and walkers, has been enjoyed by humanity throughout
the whole history of occupation in the Western Isles: archaeol-
ogists have grubbed up everything from a neolithic burial onwards.
Humps and bumps turn out to be the remains of huts and houses:
generations trip over each other in this place. At the end of the
machair path, on a windy headland with a panoramic view of the
Sound of Harris, and beyond, on a clear day, to St Kilda, stands a
small ruined twelfth-century chapel, by the circular remains of a
pagan broch. This chapel, an oblong of stone wall with a gable
sticking up at either end, is a landmark from the sea, and the focus
of the summer afternoons: 'Taking a walk out to the Temple.'
'Temple' (lest anyone jump to conclusions), though it sounds singu-
larly pagan, is the nearest English word to the Gaelic *teampuill*,

which is just a word for chapel. The green walled area is 'Pairc an Teampuill', Temple Park. 'Park' in Scotland usually means simply an enclosed field, but this one, for once, possesses some of the grace suggested by English usage; and it has a real spring, unusual in island geology, just inside the boundary wall, an improved and stone-edged spring at that, though there have been no houses here for centuries. It is the best grazing in the area, and as such reserved for the most valuable animals, rams recovering from winter business, and cows, especially when the bull is with them. At the far end of Temple Park from the spring, a rickety stile on the wall leads over to desolate slopes of rock and sparse heather, growing steeper and more barren till they end in the awesome precipice of Liuri.

Well? That's all there is to it, really, except for the atmosphere of the place. We love to go there – everyone does. For years the family walk on Sunday afternoon has been to Temple Park. But near midsummer and midwinter, I don't so much enjoy it, as feel it necessary. To be blunt (though I find it hard to believe of myself), I think I have a sneaking suspicion the sun won't do the right thing if I don't go; or that I'm giving it a hand; or showing respect, at least. Wandering out there at about the time of the winter solstice, with the twin handrests of the stile and the upthrust gables of the ruined chapel silhouetted like horns against watery sunshine, my hair stands on end and my spine prickles. A green temple garth, a sanctuary for horned beasts, a sacred spring – well, perhaps; certainly a place of refreshment. I wasn't surprised to hear that the last inhabitant of the last settlement beyond the wall was commanded by a bull-headed man who came out of the sea to forsake the place: very sensibly, she did. I thought the lifelike pink plastic phallus someone had attached to a fencepost one midwinter fitted in rather well, too, but Andrew reckoned it was in bad taste and chucked it over the cliff. I was a bit afraid retribution might follow, but no horny-headed priapic figure rose from the surf to reprimand us.

Once the sun has been duly set on its tracks again, winter changes for the better. The daily increment of afternoon light is in everyone's conversational civilities. So are the gales: the early new year often brings winds of hurricane force with the spring tides of January.

The resulting huge seas charge far beyond the normal tide-line, rolling back weakened turf in loops and spirals, and hurling sizeable rocks inland. The tidal debris contains many dead birds and a few dead sheep, as well as mounds of seaweed, which rot on the beaches to produce fertile ground for the sweet-scented white and mauve sea rocket in the summer. Such storms often reach the velocity of the one which wreaked havoc in southern England in October 1987, but since there are no trees or tall buildings to cause spectacular damage, islanders just grit their teeth and hope the roof won't blow off; but sometimes it does.

In black winter, the day following a severe gale brings more rain: in white winter, the weather may clear to calm sunshine, with a blue cloudless sky over a still-churning pine-green sea. When the wind drops away, there may be light snow and frost, and that is some of the most beautiful weather of the year. The beaches freeze down to the high-tide mark, accentuating every rimed shell and seaweed stalk with long violet shadows. Against the dazzling whiteness, the intertidal sand glows intensely pink or golden, darker than the pastel jade and turquoise of the sea. The old worn hills look as bright and clean-cut as Alps, the faded winter dunes are new and wonderful, sparkling white, scribed in blue arcs and circles by compass-points of marram turning in the wind. Snow and frost are not familiars of this wet maritime region, but when they come, they grace it with unexpected beauties. A thin freezing wind blowing across the glittering beach rolls tiny particles of snow before it, turning and turning them on the miles of flat sand till they grow to walnuts, then apples, then footballs of snow, skidding along with a dry whisper of sound, in an intricate mysterious game of ball. The quicksand of black winter hardens, desiccates and leaves layered and faulted ice veined with sand like pyrites over an empty hole. If you break the ice, the wind catches the fragments and curls them across the smooth surface with a high ringing like the tone of a glass harp. The spring-tide-filled lagoon freezes at dusk into small beads, then floes, then sheets, gathering and clashing before the icy wind, pressing with fearsome glee round wading ankles. Ravens exult, flagrantly black: so many sheep have lain down to die, so many little living morsels have gone numb and silly and easy to mop up. The rabbits are dozy with cold, and dazzled: even a very clumsy Labrador has a chance of catching one, and a great many fleas along with it.

Frozen moonlight is best for catching stupefied rabbits. Jet in his prime used to get us out of bed two or three times a night to the chase during the full moons of January and February. The moon is powerful then, warring palely with the sun by day, and triumphant by night, haloed and vibrant, scattering the stars to the farthest horizon. Small wonder if it turns a canine brain to werewolf fantasies.

It takes a moonless night to reveal that even more uncanny brightness, the Northern Lights. They are there all the time, faintly visible on clear nights as a faint arc of pallor on the northern horizon, except when summer afterglow or bright moonlight outshines them; but the best displays are in early and late winter, October and February. It takes time for the eye bludgeoned by electric light to adjust to their pale shimmering and pulsing, but if you have the patience to stand outside in the dark long enough to notice them, it is difficult to tear yourself away. Searchlight beams and waving curtains of white, greenish and pinkish light, brightening and fading in different rhythms, may cover three-quarters of the sky, as endlessly changing and yet the same as ripples in flowing water. There is a Celtic legend that the Northern Lights, like the fairies, were once angels; but after the war in Heaven, God found that though he had got rid of the Evil One and his followers, there were still elements among his celestials which, if not against him, were not for him either. These spirits he demoted to the world of men, where they still dance airily in angelic beauty.

A spell of white weather has more mundane surprises too. We have Flopsy, Mopsy, Cottontail and Peter and dozens of their cousins living in our field outside the garden walls, but we always try to think well of them, so that it is something of a shock to see proof on a snowy morning that the whole tribe use our garden paths as highways, and that the parsley, carnations and sweet williams disappeared for reasons other than bad weather. Also, it becomes painfully obvious that the small mouse which has been climbing up inside the walls every evening from the old rainwater drains is actually a rather large rat: or perhaps several large rats. And the neighbours' bloodthirsty cats have been up again, paying no attention to rats or rabbits, but terrorising blackbirds. The signatures left by contemptuous vermin in the snow are always demoralising. Of course we wouldn't harm any of them, but why do the horrible brutes realise that? They're obviously piling in from miles around.

The snowy beach has its messages too, with less embarrassing loading. Tracks difficult to pick out in soft dry sand are eye-catching in the snow. What we most love to see are otter tracks; what we most dislike, the prints of mink: two superficially similar mustelids, one native, the other an escapee from a fur farm of the 1950s. Otter's prints are round and honest, he slides with abandon in the snow, runs up every mound and hummock, for the pleasure of jumping off again, bounces up to every new piece of flotsam out of sheer curiosity. Mink's light long-fingered prints are mean and stealthy, his path murderously straight, his only stops to scent-mark, leaving threatening messages. Or perhaps it is only partiality which decodes things in this way, for feral mink now suffer from the exaggerated opprobrium that used to be directed at the otter, until declining numbers and great publicity jobs like *Tarka the Otter* and *Ring of Bright Water* invested the latter with as much poignant glamour as the panda: we always seem to like a species better when we have got it thoroughly licked. But as late as the 1950s otters were being accused of killing lambs: and their attested depredations up to that date had included not only desirable fish, but poultry, full-grown sheep, and even grain! There may come a time to deride the accusations now thrown at feral mink – that they kill poultry for fun, only drinking the blood, and leaving the corpses; that they will murder a bird as big as a full-grown goose; that they drive out otters and eat their cubs. However, I am pretty sure the mink, which is a fast breeder and a bold opportunist, will never decline in numbers as the slow-maturing, retiring otter has; and as long as mink are around in large numbers, they will be regarded as vermin, like rats and crows and other chancers. In this connection, it is worth noting that even now the otter's claims to public affection and untarnished virtue hold only where people can't by the most extreme stretch of paranoia imagine that otters interfere with human health or wealth: but think what has happened to badgers in areas where they might conceivably be (but almost certainly aren't) a link in the spread of bovine tuberculosis; and in the west of Scotland, where otters are commonest, they too are shot without a second thought by fish farmers (sorry, by the predator control officers attached to fish farms).

So the mink's lurid reputation may well stay with it. In a non-pejorative way, it is deserved: mink by nature take many birds as prey, like the pine marten, weasel and stoat with which they have much in common. This being the case, it isn't surprising that, as an introduced species, it is now wiping out colonies of ground-nesting birds which have never had to face such a predator; and 'ground-nesting' includes poor silly hens in henhouses. Of course, this is not the mink's fault, but man's, as with any other introduced or escaped 'pest'. Just a pity that it's other species which have to suffer the consequence: if it were human throats mink went for, we might be more careful.

I believe that the claim that all mink are bloodthirsty killers for fun is much exaggerated: it is more likely that some mink (like some stoats, weasels, foxes, dogs, and humans) work themselves up into a killing frenzy, and such animals are bound to regard a henhouse as a sporting enthusiast's paradise. But if a mink ever killed otter cubs, it must have been a real berserker, heedless of all danger, for even a small female otter is four times as heavy as the largest mink, and they are protective mothers. In fact, in Russia, the opposite accusation is levelled – that otters kill mink, which are there valued for their skins! The otter's decline at last attracted sympathy just at the time when feral mink were blossoming in Britain, but it is by now fairly clear that the otter's only enemy is man: the trapping and hunting of earlier centuries had caused a population crash anyway, and this was dramatically exacerbated by destruction of suitable habitat and the use of organochlorides such as Deildrin, which were ingested from prey, and caused infertility. That mink and otters can coexist is abundantly clear in this area: at least two small islands we know (very confined spaces) have both mink burrows and an otter holt.

With wild birds, it is a different matter. There is no doubt at all that once mink have bred to capacity in any small area, they can totally banish bird life. This was impressed on me last year in the

Strond and Renish area of Harris – a long peninsula which used to support large nesting colonies of gulls, terns and waders 'before we got the mink', as anyone local will tell you. I went to count breeding birds, and on a three-mile stretch of coastline, I found a few wheatears and rock pipits, and a single pair of hoodies with only one chick – and evidence of countless mink. The peat was riddled with burrows and strewn with scats, which contained few bird remains – they must have eaten themselves out of that food supply. At one point, a very young mink emerged a few feet from me, and in fact came towards me when I imitated its chittering: then the pointed little face broke into a cat-like snarl and it ambled unsteadily away. We know at least two islands which used to have many breeding birds, where burgeoning mink population has made it not worth while for any bird to attempt nesting. On the other hand, where mink are present but not numerous, we have found their burrows a few hundred yards from thriving colonies of terns and gulls. Even there, they may well oust the birds eventually, as they are capable of breeding at a year old, produce young at least yearly, and up to sixteen in a litter. Certainly in the situations I have mentioned they were preying on the nearby colonies: we found terns, a black guillemot, a young shag and a young but fully grown greater blackback pulled forcibly down mink burrows by the head, this last bird quite a feat for an animal that weighs four pounds at most. But in spite of their small size – under two feet from nose to tail-tip – mink give an impression of steely sinew and total determination in all their movements. If you meet a mink at close quarters, it will stand up and brazen it out, fleeing only at the last minute; and if you are not pursuing but merely standing by, they will continue about their business with complete indifference. If cats or dogs investigate them too closely, they will fight fiercely: if the other party is a cat, it may end up dead.

In this liking for a fight, as in so much else, the mink is quite different from the otter, which prefers to make itself scarce unobtrusively, but if disturbed at close range will usually bolt with no more than an exasperated hiss – though I have seen one wallop Jet's nose when he attempted to force indecent attentions on her.

Inexperienced otter spotters may occasionally think they have seen an otter when it was in fact a mink. The best way to make the difference obvious is perhaps to liken the mink to a ferret or polecat. It is slightly larger, and chocolate-brown to black in colour, but the general gait, the proportion of long slender body to short rather bushy tail, and the pointed face with its alert round ears and eyes are quite reminiscent of these smaller mustelids. The otter, by comparison, as well as being nearly twice the length, appears more beavery or doggy than weaselly, with a broad muzzle, round head, stout legs, broad webbed feet, and a long tail very thick at the base and pointed at the tip, which acts as an efficient rudder. Even a very young, mink-sized otter has this characteristic tail. Though otter coat-colour varies between individuals, the usual impression is of a chestnut-brown animal slightly lighter on the underside. In the water, mink swim fast and purposefully in a straight line, whereas otters take their time and take the air. They may loop through the water surfacing three or four times a minute to breathe, showing a rounded back in between; or float for a while on the back or side, turning leisurely from one position to another, watching passing boats with curiosity. If frightened, or in pursuit of fish, they dive, showing tail-tip last. Like seals, they give a subtle impression of having plenty of spare time, and enjoying every minute of it. Whether an otter is sleeping in the sun, crunching up a crab, idling in the water, taking a short cut down a slippery bank, or squirming in the grass to get dry, there is a powerful sense that that particular action, and that particular way of performing that action, was chosen out of sheer *joie de vivre*. Dour scientific opinion has it that in the wild only very young otters or courting couples 'play' – and of course, don't forget the inverted commas round 'play'; humans play, other creatures 'play'. What the scientists forget (perhaps because they so seldom see the subjects of their research in the wild) is that even the most routine chores can be turned into play by someone of a cheerful disposition: that was the point of human work-songs in the days when people still sang them. The wisecracks of postmen and barmen, the exaggerated horsing of builder's labourers, the solitary dancesteps of a housewife with the radio on, are not exactly play – but what else are they? Whatever else they are, otters are doing it, too. *And* they play, brazenly and unashamedly, when they should be performing hunting behaviour, or territorial behaviour, or some other behaviour of a sort prescribed for otters by scientists: I have seen an adult wild otter rushing down a slippery weed-covered rock into the water, bounding up to the top again, and sliding and splashing time after time with an expression of the utmost glee.

We are very lucky to be able to see otters as frequently as we do. The north and west of Scotland are the only parts of Britain where they are relatively common, and where they venture out during the day. Add to this the lack of cover, and the fact that in the sea the otter feels completely safe, and we have unrivalled opportunities for watching otters behaving naturally. We have seldom gone to particular places or sat waiting to see otters – watchers who are more systematic in an area like this can glean a wealth of knowledge. Most of our sightings of otters are from the boat: otters on land are more discreet. All the same they are hardly the shy creatures they are sometimes painted: we quite often see them off Leverburgh pier, and Andrew and Sarah came across one actually in Leverburgh village, eating a fish on the shore by the mainroad, unconcerned by the nasty little boys who were chucking stones at it. I imagine otters learn by experience, and pass the knowledge through generations, as the young spend up to a year with the mother; otters in this region may therefore be less wary than elsewhere, as they suffered comparatively little persecution in the past, though they were killed as occasion arose when times were lean and pelts were in demand. It was landowners and their gamekeepers who hated otters most, and they were themselves a class not much loved by the islanders. I get the impression that in these coastal regions, the otter was never regarded as vermin, at least until the fish farmers came along.

In spite of the Hebridean otter's comparative unwariness, we see their tracks much more often than themselves. Every freshwater stream giving onto a soft beach displays daily tracks, as the animals lie up along the burns and fish in the sea. Usually we see prints of single adults, or of a mother with one or two young: this latter is the typical family group, living in a territory overlapping a male otter's, but not coinciding with it completely. Otters may breed at any time of year, but not always every year; so at any season we are on the look-out for the two sets of adult prints which could indicate a mating couple. We have seen such prints side by side on a frosty February beach, running together for a couple of miles. That would mean cubs in May: a good time to be born.

The courting otters' tracks in the bright snow of February remind that spring is already a possibility. It was a medieval belief that the birds chose their mates on St Valentine's day, and I think maybe the Harris birds still do.

Chapter 15

The Weather the Raven Loves

The raven loves clear calm weather at any time of year, but most of all in February. Their Valentine messages are spelt out in living black arabesques against a pale blue sky. It may be the twentieth season these long-lived monogamous couples have spiralled and kronked above their nest-sites, but not for them the perfunctory kiss-on-the-way-out-the-door. The ravens' epithalamium is new every year.

The dismal weather of earlier winter spoils the raven's fun. Not that it is a lean time; there is a daily feast of sheep carrion from October onwards, so that ravens are in full-fed breeding condition when many other birds are struggling to keep going. But like those other intelligent carnivores, seals and otters, ravens have a lot of spare time to fill in between their nourishing and easily-got meals. Short days, misty skies and high winds don't create a shortage of food, but they do deprive ravens of entertainment. Their hobby is flying: they like to soar on an updraught, drop with folded wings, brake and shoot off to right or left; they perform vertical corkscrews, sideways rolls, back somersaults, lateral spirals and wingtip-to-wingtip synchronised versions of all their tricks. They like plenty of space, to show off in front of their fellows, and to be able to keep in touch vocally and visually over long distances. Bad weather thwarts ravens as surely as it does gardeners or dinghy sailors.

Ravens play in the air all the year round except when they are too burdened by nesting duties to spare the time. There is a period between April and early June when we always wonder what has happened to the ravens. We miss the carrying 'kruk-kruk-kruk' high up above the noise of the other birds – the call that means 'Here I am – come with me.' And the birds themselves, if we see them at all, fly low and furtively, without their characteristic swagger. We are always afraid of persecution at that time, ever since we found the female of a long-established pair shot dead on her nest, in a steep gully overhung by scrub willow, impossible for any predator, man or mink, to reach, but a sitting target for a gunman ten yards away on the opposite lip. The raven is, of course, officially protected, but official protection in the highlands and islands is worth about as much as an umbrella in the Kalahari. The owners of neglected sheep which lose lambs are often on the look-out for a scapegoat, and ravens, like buzzards and eagles, are obvious enough victims to be easy to hit. In fact, ravens do not kill healthy lambs: they take placentas, stillbirths and lambs that have died of starvation. The hoody crow will take live newborn lambs as well, if they are unattended, as they frequently are; but the man who is too lazy to care for his lambing ewes is unlikely to trouble himself about which bird is a menace and which is not.

Perhaps some ravens are sufficiently worldly wise to know this, and to keep a low profile during the lambing season, when they are themselves busy feeding young. Ravens are certainly intelligent enough to adjust their behaviour to prevailing conditions: fifty years ago, when they were harried not just by an occasional gunslinger but by every gamekeeper in the country, they were extremely wary birds, nesting only on remote moorland or seashore cliffs. Now that few people here bother them, they are commonly seen feeding boldly on roads and rubbish tips – except during those spring months. But there may be other reasons for their temporary absence: perhaps they are keeping unfledged or newly-fledged families hidden from neighbour ravens or are too busy carrying food to loiter with intent in accustomed gathering places; or perhaps territory is so strictly defined at that important season that ravens flying across others' territories must adopt a mien that says 'just passing through'.

Whatever the truth of it is, ravens bounce back again late in the summer, and by September the young are as skilled and agile in the air as their parents. All the aerobatic exercises seen in courtship are practised by the young families too; it is a wonderful sight to see ten or twelve of these huge jet black birds – black from beak to tail and poll to claw – soaring, plummeting, rolling and spiralling round each other with a buoyancy of movement which suggests the unseen strings of a puppet show. Birds on the ground or flying between manoeuvres call the repeated sonorous 'kruk' of contact, sometimes keeping up a conversation between three or four different hillsides, over distances of two miles or more. Birds in pairs about to perform a special trick, particularly the double lateral roll, call out a rhythmical gurgling 'killik-kollok', a sound rather like the last bit of water belching back over an air bubble from an emptying sink: 'Now look at this!' Whether such pairs are always mated or intending to mate, I don't know. It is possible: the displaying groups one sees from late summer onwards are usually bigger than the six to eight of a normal raven nuclear family. If several families tend to meet up, it would not be unlikely that the youngsters would select partners and contract 'engagements' which will lead to eventual mating: bearded tits, wandering albatrosses, greylags and various other monogamists do this. On the other hand, it is just as probable that this exuberant flying is not solely sexual in reference, but an expression of solidarity, like the triumph-calling of greylags, which cements the family bond. In that case, the larger groups might well be composed of blood relatives nesting near each other, with their offspring: nesting next door to brothers and fathers has been noticed in great tits, and may well be the norm in some other less studied species. Whatever the truth may be, the autumn gatherings of ravens, even when assembled for a serious purpose, break up into exuberant gymnas-tics at the least excuse. Ten or fifteen ravens hunched round a road-casualty mutton like so many mourners may suddenly take off, circle, and perform a gleeful aerial dance, some bounding high in the air while others plummet, so that for two or three enormous loops the highest and lowest points of the communal flight synchronise like juggler's clubs. The same gratuitous expenditure of energy – there can really be no other explanation except that it's fun – takes place when a raven is seeing off a buzzard or eagle from the nesting territory. The defending bird will roll and wheel and tip the invader's wings and cocoon him in swift close spirals till he is sick and dizzy and can think of nothing but getting into the next thermal and thence away on longer wings. The raven will pursue for some distance, jeering and rollicking. Then back to his wife and family, and there is a raven jig of triumph, with much croaking, popping and gurgling.

Ravens are ready to join in any argument, even if it is not directly theirs. Recently in Mull we saw a family of three hungry eagles entering the territory of a larger family of six buzzards. The dialogue was fairly understated, because of the laziness of buzzards, until a clan of twelve ravens flew in from the next hillside. They mobbed all the other birds at random, which could be taken as an instinctive blind reaction to large raptors, were it not for the exaggerated enjoyment they seemed to derive from the occasion, breaking off for fancy aerobatics together and totally bewildering both the resident buzzards and the invading eagles. When the fun was over, the ravens simply flew off, laughing horribly.

These communal antics alter subtly as the days begin to lengthen in late winter. The movements and calls are the same, but intensely concentrated between pairs. Sometimes another bird or two will try to join in; the conventional theory is that this is a rival male vying for a female, but as ravens retain the same partners for life this seems unlikely, except for very young birds. More often, the gooseberry is probably one of the previous year's offspring, since the birds have been cavorting in family groups for the past half year. In support of this theory – which is pure speculation on my part – I have noticed that the mated pair, rolling and spiralling together and flying side by side, wing to wing, at first tend to ignore the intruder – very unlike their behaviour with rivals who invade their territory. Only when the third party's boisterous behaviour makes it impossible for the partners to synchronise their dance does the male turn and give chase in exasperation.

I have said that the calls and movements of courtship are the same as in other seasons, and this is true, but even to a human observer it is clear that the sense is now different. The pair fly close together, responding intently to each other's slightest movement. There is none of the spontaneous clowning of autumn. The impression is of intense, ecstatic, disciplined precision: not a disco any more, but a ballet. I have lain on my back in thin February snow till I almost froze to it, watching the ravens' nuptial dance, passages of controlled spiralling and rolling high against the strengthening blue of a sky promising spring; then a long glissade side by side in perfect time against the white hillside; the female soars upwards again in a graceful arc while her partner circles her in widening loops, hanging motionless for a moment at the top of each curve of movement; then he throws himself into the air, and bounds away with the 'kronk-kronk-kronk' which indicates raven good humour, swooping low to the ground in a sudden relaxation of formal gravity: now he is apt to show off, and clown and be his usual raven self. You can make a raven in that mood swoop over your head on great creaking wings by calling 'kronk' at him, and once one particularly roguish bird zoomed to within a foot of poor Jet's bumbling black head, to his great alarm. The raven flew off chortling.

So the ravens call it spring already, when frost is still plaguing the garden sparrows and snow is still killing sheep. They are about the earliest nesters of all the birds. A Gaelic proverb has it, 'Nest at Candlemas, egg at Shrovetide, bird at Easter, otherwise the raven has death.' The Popish festivals mentioned indicate a pre-Reformation saying, but the raven wouldn't be bothered anyway: he is an out-and-out heathen, Odin's bird. The crafty shapeshifting king of the gods had two ravens, Thought and Memory, who ranged the world every day, and returned to Valhalla at suppertime, to share in the feast and give their master all the gossip. The Norsemen respected the raven's strength, intelligence and cunning; tame ravens were often carried in Viking longships, so that like Noah's bird they could be let loose to find land. It was said to have been a raven which discovered Iceland in this manner. Ravens often featured on Norse war-banners: whether the raven emblem appeared to flap or droop was taken as a sign for the day. Among less war-like people, the raven has usually been regarded askance, as a bird of ill omen:

> 'The boding raven on her cottage sat
> And with hoarse croaking warned us of our fate.'

But Vikings were less lily-livered. To be followed by a raven on the way to a fight (and Vikings were usually on the way to a fight) was a lucky sign: the raven expected the warrior to provide him with carrion. Norse fighters evidently didn't expect to become carrion themselves, though a raven would hardly be particular about which side in a conflict he ate.

This superstition survived well into the present century among west highland deer-stalkers. A raven overhead at setting out meant a successful hunt. This is not so daft: an experienced old raven might well be able to make a fair judgment based on who is shooting, prevailing weather conditions, and location of deer.

Come to think of it, the same might be true in raven appreciation of fighting ability: follow that man with the very effective Constantinople mailcoat, or that crazy-looking chap with no clothes on at all – they're the most likely to bring 'em in. But for the general rabble of ravens not particularly gifted with the wisdom of age, it is more likely they just went along to see what was doing. Ravens don't like to miss out on any fracas, being in this respect rather like Vikings themselves.

That prognostication of a successful kill was not the only legacy the Norsemen left. Though the islands of the west were not as thoroughly colonised or for as long a period as the Orkneys and Shetland, nevertheless from the ninth to the thirteenth centuries they were Norsemen's country, so much so that the Scots called them 'Innsigal' – the foreigners' islands. Eighty per cent of Lewis and Harris place names are Scandinavian in origin, many ending in the elements -sta, -bost, -shader (from stathr, bolstathr, saetr), denoting a farm, the principal farm in a township, and an out-pasture. A new settler was entitled to all the land within a knife's throw of his *stathr*, dividing it into home-pasture and out-pasture, so that the first element in such place names is usually the settler's own name. One place name reveals a less peaceful story – Luskentyre, from the Gaelic *loisig an tir*, 'they burned the dwellings.' This is probably an allusion to the ferocious purge of Magnus Bareleg of Norway in 1098, to reassert Norwegian sovereignty over the too-independent jarldom of Man and the Isles. It is still remembered that he destroyed all the Hebridean woodlands, which evidence in the peat shows once existed. A spell of colder climate following on Magnus's devastation ensured that they never grew again bigger than scrub. Latterly sheep have demolished even that. Yet though sheep themselves are now sacrosanct in Hebridean eyes, time was when they too were regarded as a scourge. More than seven centuries after Magnus, the proprietors of that same Luskentyre cleared the whole fertile west side of Harris to make a sheep-run of it. The tenants of nearby Crago served with notices of eviction couldn't believe it, until they saw the redcoats enter and once more burn the dwellings. When Stewart of Luskentyre asked his wife, who was behind the scheme, if she was happy now the people had been evicted, she replied that she would not be happy as long as there was hearth-smoke to be seen between Luskentyre and Rodel. The most rumbustious Viking could scarcely have bettered these words of the upright Christian lady of the age of enlightenment.

But the ravens who chortled over Magnus's butchery kept right on laughing. Where there are sheep there will soon be feasting, fleece to line the nest, and shank bones to make it pretty. An ill wind that blows nobody good! What better for a raven, than to scribe the blue sky with amorous calligraphy, while cold numbs the old ewes slowly into mutton?

Chapter 16

A Bird for All Seasons

'What are those birds?'

There's always a chance of seeing something unusual when you land on an uninhabited island, some exhausted passager, perhaps, or a rare species which has been quietly breeding unsuspected and undisturbed. But nine times out of ten, the answer to the hopeful question is 'Starlings!'

Starlings are everywhere: exploiters of every food source, denizens of every habitat, mimics of every voice, shifters of shape and colour. The half dozen dark little birds flitting low across a windswept channel are not Leach's petrels; the indistinct flock spiralling down on a distant skerry are not an exciting collection of newly-arrived migrant waders; the two squat forms glimpsed between intertidal boulders are not purple sandpipers thinking of breeding. In dazzling light, in murky conditions, from a moving boat, just round a corner, those birds will turn out to be starlings. I suppose we have never really got used to seeing these most vulgar and verminous of birds in such sublime surroundings. Other birds have liquid haunting voices, flight as graceful as the wind, sea-clean plumage – but starlings! They wheeze and waddle and squabble and chitter on the jewel-bright pasture of Saghay or the salt-scoured brow of Shillay's terrible cliffs with no more decorum than on the garden grass at home. Poke, squawk, bounce in the air – off the cliff edge, over the dreadful Atlantic swells, as if it were a farmyard puddle.

In fact, they are quite right. This is their country, and a very good place to be for starlings. The present widespread and numerous starling population of mainland Britain is a relatively recent phenomenon. In the early nineteenth century they were not particularly common, except in the Northern and Western Isles. Here the subspecies *zetlandicus* was already thoroughly at home. Far from finding themselves hampered by lack of trees, dour climate, and paucity of grain and berries, island starlings thrive, nesting in rock crevices and drystone walls, scavenging the shores for dead fish and small invertebrates, and the hills for sheep carrion and attendant maggots. Indeed, a sheep need not be carrion to be of service to starlings; they are often to be seen lined up on the backs of grazing animals, pecking parasites out of the fleece, or just leaping up and down screeching because the back of a sheep is a nice perch.

Starlings are our most ubiquitous birds. Sparrows and blackbirds are only common round houses with gardens, and other 'garden' birds hardly occur at all, while the twites, pipits and all the larger birds are wary of human habitation; but starlings are equally at home in town, on the crofts, or on the smallest offshore islands. Last summer I surveyed our local area for the British Trust for Ornithology's new atlas of breeding birds. In twenty-six hours and as many square kilometres of hill, moor, saltings, freshwater lochs cliffs and estuary, I found starlings in every kilometre square, all breeding insouciantly, not to say incessantly, for our starlings nearly always raise two broods, and often squeeze in a third; so the importunate wheezy clamour of the nestlings is audible almost anywhere you care to listen below about the 100-metre contour, all the time between April and late July.

Any cranny of the right size invites a starling to set up home, apparently. When we first came to Harris, we were puzzled to notice that several rural postboxes had had scarves tied round the apertures, which had to be lifted to post letters. These were nest sites much coveted by starlings. Metal surroundings are always highly esteemed, though you would imagine they would produce problems of heat and cold, and be appallingly noisy in rain; but since starlings seem to like noise and usually make as much as possible themselves this latter might be a positive attraction. Happily for starlings, the island is littered with abandoned cars and old oildrums, some in extraordinary positions half way up steep hills or in the middle of remote belts of sand dunes. Every single one of them chirps and wheezes lustily throughout the summer.

Starlings are very faithful to their nest-sites. For each of the thirteen years we have lived here, a pair of starlings has raised two or three broods in a crevice by our gate onto the main road, using our signboard as a singing post, to the detriment of the paintwork. They are a careless couple: we often find a stray egg lying a few yards from their door, an incongruously delicate early-morning-blue egg for such an untidy ragbag of a bird. Of course, it is possible that the lost egg may be evidence of good housekeeping rather than bad, if the parents can recognise any which are infertile or contain dead chicks. Near to hatching, they might do this from small noises made by live chicks inside the viable eggs.

Certainly starlings can be very decided about such matters once the nestlings are hatched. We have three other regular nests under the eaves of a single-storey shed which we use for storage. Finding one day that a weak but still live hatchling had (as we thought) fallen out onto the wall-plate, we replaced it. Half an hour later, the runt was turfed out again by its unsentimental parents.

We have always assumed that 'our' starlings are the same pairs every year. Various studies with ringed birds have shown, however, that though starlings occasionally live into their twenties, the vast majority survive for only one or two breeding seasons; and that though normally monogamous for each brood, the territorial males may change mates every season or sometimes between clutches, and that some even have a wife under every gutter. These variable marital habits seem to arise from the starling's unshakable conviction that the purpose of life is to increase and multiply. If the wife of the moment spends too much time feeding to regain strength between broods, or helping the fledged young to forage, the husband may feel it his duty to start afresh, like Henry VIII. Where food is extremely plentiful, birds may live longer and pairs may stay together longer.

Our acre and a half of ground, teeming with garden insect life, with a frequently replenished bird table, hen's corn scattered every day, and plenty of dead sheep on the hill behind, is a pretty good environment for starlings: it may well be that our residents survive particularly well, and perhaps their marriages do, too. Certainly, the oldest site, near the gate, has the singing proprietor present at intervals through the winter, and there is often a second bird with him, presumably the current mate. The south-facing site in the shed has a singing-post on the ridge above, and this bird – or *a* bird – is there all through the year, and has been for about eight years. I think it is the same bird, because he is a particularly good mimic. He is responsible for the cat on the electricity wires, the buzzard in the carpark, the pony in the front garden, the shepherd on the roof and numerous other curiosities, and his whole performance can often be heard from the shed roof-ridge. Throughout this past autumn his last brood seemed to keep him company, and since he is still sitting at his post with three other birds in late winter, I wonder if starlings recognise family groups. If so, it may well be that the remaining two nest sites in that shed, which appeared a year and two years after the south-facing one, belong to sons of the oldest inhabitant. Nest inheritance from father to son could also explain seeming longevity.

These four regular nests provide us with most entertainment, as the inhabitants are so used to human presence; but there must be a dozen or so other starling nests in our garden walls and the old range of outbuildings. This long line of byres and stables, with its rusty corrugated iron roof, has been ripe for renovation for a long time now, and probably always will be. Andrew spent a lot of time and effort clearing the nameless and noisome rubbish of past generations out of the largest shed in the row and reroofed it, to make a weathertight store for keeping building timber and dismantled bits of boat in. As well as weathertight, it was to be starling proof – for years he had suffered from messy droppings on every bit of wood he worked with. Wherever he kept his timber, starlings seemed to be roosting above it. This time, they would be totally excluded, he vowed. The floor was swept, the timber cleaned off, and the roof finished nice and tightly – except for one small hole to humour the blackbird who had watched it all from her nest in the rafters. The hundred or so starlings who had used the tie beams as a roost when the roof was in rags and tatters were not to be humoured. For a day or so at sunset they crowded disconsolately on to the ridge, wheezing and exclaiming, then were seen no more. We left the blackbirds in peace for a time, feeling they had had enough disturbance during re-roofing. But when eventually Andrew needed some timber, he discovered that that one small hole was as handy for a hundred starlings as for two blackbirds. He covered the defiled wood with polythene, and swore that the hole should be closed, as the young blackbirds were out of the nest. But then the nest was found to contain a second clutch, and then we grew too busy to bother, and then it was autumn, and it seemed cruel to send poor starlings off in the wind and rain to find new roosts. Somehow that shed never was made starling proof.

We had a starling problem in the house as well, though at the time we blamed that other embarrassing occasional tenant, the rat. One evening Andrew came through from serving dinner looking drawn and anxious. 'There's a rat in the wall through there, clumping around in jackboots.' He glared at me. I always get the blame for rats. 'People are bound to hear it.'

'Don't you dare poison it!'

'That poison is perfectly humane.'

'Remember the last one.' The last one died behind the arras, as it were, and could be nosed as you went up to the stairs into the lobby. Dead rats are very much more unpleasant than live rats. 'Anyway,' I added, for good measure, 'they don't like the poison.'

Neither they do. Once they've seen what it did to weak-minded Cousin Randolph they won't touch it.

We thought the rat might leave quietly in the night, but not so. Breakfast was taken to the accompaniment of thumping, scrabbling and scuffling. Andrew talked a great deal very loudly, and people at least pretended not to notice anything odd. When he had finally hustled the last guest out of the dining room, he called me through to listen. Suddenly I remembered the noise from the seasonal sounds in the roof-space above my bedroom when I was a girl.

'That's not a rat, it's a starling.'

'Starling my foot! It's a rat.'

'No, that's it flapping its wings.'

'A winged rat.'

But finally he agreed that even if it had flown there, it was now stuck somehow in a section of wall between battens, about three feet by two; and that it couldn't be left there to starve miserably on the other side of a partition from a crowd of gross munching diners.

'We'll just have to take the hardboard off,' I said. 'We were going to put plasterboard there anyway.'

'And how do we get the plasterboard up, papered and painted before dinner time?'

I insisted that people would understand and that if they didn't they could go to hell, and set off to find the wrecking bar. But Andrew, more intelligently, armed himself with a jig saw, removed a painting of barnyard fowls from the area where the winged rat

187

was fluttering, and cut a round hole the size of an orange. It revealed a scrawny leg with frozen claws clutched round a batten. Squinting in sideways, we could just make out the frowsty brownish plumage and terrified eye of a juvenile starling, which must have fallen down inside the wall-space from a nest under the eaves or in one of the old cracked chimneys. The hole was much too narrow to get a hand in. Waving titbits and making starling noises did no good at all. Eventually we opened both windows wide, laid a plate of raw mince conspicuously on a table, and left the room. That worked: when we dared to look half an hour later, our winged rat had gone. We hung the barnyard fowls back over the hole. That was five years ago, and there is still a starling-sized hole under the picture. It might come in handy again some time.

We wouldn't be without our chortling, squabbling, swaggering starlings for anything. How often in the middle of a dull day spent scurrying from chore to chore they make us jump and then laugh, with the incongruous sounds of a curlew, an eagle, a herring gull close by our ears. What glee they show in their spring nest refurbishments, what cheerful optimism in the midwinter morning twilight, hopping up and down in anticipation of bird-table breakfast when they see the lights go on. Whatever the weather, like the poor they are always with us, importunate, impudent, raucous, screeching vulgar hand-me-down ballads, scratching like scabby urchins, capering, jostling, scrapping. Forget the Leach's petrels. Starlings, that's what those birds are.

Afterword

Of course, on the only occasion when the starlings flitting past the mast did turn out to be Leach's petrels, we were exultant. Rarities unexpectedly seen, and still more the hope of seeing them, add a certain excitement to the most routine walk or boat trip.

But having said that, it seems to me that no walk, still less any boat trip, is ever routine. It is a recurrent wonder just to be present in the everyday, ever-changing surroundings of sea and islands, as well known to us as our own hands, as unpredictable as dreams; where common creatures go about their ordinary lives, whose habits become so familiar that we begin to feel we understand what it is to be a grey seal or a blackback. But as familiarity grows, it changes its character. Recognition, yes: it is a boost to confidence to be able to tell an arctic tern from a common, a juvenile eagle from an adult, the postures of aggression from those of courtship. But ultimately, where does all this naming of parts lead? Only to further questions. To say 'A Leach's petrel!' feels in itself a bit of a triumph: so rare, so like the pictures in the books. But to say a 'A starling!' is quite different: past the stage of pictures in books, what do we know? Why does the bird do this, or that, rather than something else? What is it conscious of, how does its world articulate? What *is* it like to be a starling, or a grey seal, or a blackback?

Identification, prediction, cannot of themselves take the mystery from common things. The familiar progress of the year remains mysterious; when the sun sets again north of Toe Head into the sea on the twenty-third of April, or behind Gasker on Midsummer Day, it does just what I expect, but I am baffled. Though I have a smattering of twentieth-century physics and can learn the answer to 'How?' if I look up the right books, I am just as full of 'Why?' as the remote people who placed the standing stones on our headlands. And all the creatures who keep their times and tempos according to their own perceptions of that one sun remain mysterious, even – perhaps especially – the most common.

Most of us probably puzzle from time to time over the vagaries of humanity. Frequently, some aspect of history or some current story in the news makes us stop and ponder: what are people thinking of? Why do they act like that? What is it to be human, faced with that choice, those circumstances? When it comes to workmates, friends, relatives, lovers, spouses, the questioning becomes a constant, almost unnoticed, background to everything we do or say together: what mood, what motive? We need to understand these things at every turn to make a relationship meaningful. Without the questions, whether internal or overt – Do you like this? Would you prefer that? What is he thinking? Why is she nervous? – the Other remains unknown, a shadow puppet in our private fantasy world. We can recognise a stranger from a photograph, a description, a badge of office; but recognising our friends is a much subtler business, requiring continuous effort at many levels.

I think most of my readers would agree that we need to extend this sensitivity outwards to include humans who are not our friends; and then – at any rate, so I believe – to others who are not human. The Leach's petrel, like the Queen, is so seldom seen that we may be forced to give up on it. But for creatures more common in our environment, we can cultivate that attitude of alertness which we practise towards our friends, instead of stifling it with 'It's not important' or 'They're only animals.' A child says, 'My puppy's crying'; a family at the zoo watching chimps exclaim 'Ooh, don't they look human!'; a parrot's owner claims his pet understands 'every word'; a researcher cultivates cancer in mice as 'an animal model' for the study of sarcomata in humans. All these people are claiming, in different ways, 'Animals are like us.'

But put it as a question, 'Are they like us?' and the answer 'yes' becomes too embarrassing to contemplate; because if they *are* like us, in many of the ways in which we are like each other, we perhaps owe them more consideration than we show – the sort of consideration that (at least in principle) we allow fellow members of our own species.

Put the question another way. Are we different? If so, how? Watching other animals go about their daily lives yields some answers, and further questions.

What makes my own life worth living? Some of the answers are: social intercourse with familiar individuals, sufficient food, warmth and shelter, freedom of physical movement. If these basic requirements were taken away, life would only be worthwhile if I could hope for their return. Any 'higher' values (except perhaps for a few rare saints or scholars) can only be realised if built on these foundations. I do not see much difference between the bases of my own and other people's happiness, and those of a raven's or a seal's. To a large extent, the higher values are frills. The thousand books on my shelves will not console me if my husband dies or if I am starving. There is some emotional top growth in human language, arts, religion, ethics, but the roots of emotion are in our animal nature; and without emotion, without love, joy, fear, grief, hope, we would not be able to care what happened to us. There would be no zest to life – no *human* life as we understand it.

So to the question 'Are they like us?' I would answer 'Yes, in most of the things that matter; because we are like them.'

How could we live otherwise?

BY THE SAME AUTHOR

A House by the Shore

Scarista Style

First published in Great Britain 1989
by Victor Gollancz Ltd
14 Henrietta Street, London WC2E 8QJ

Text © Alison Johnson 1989
Illustrations © John Busby 1989

British Library Cataloguing in Publication Data
Johnson, Alison
 Islands in the Sound.
 1. Scotland. Hebrides. Animals.
 I. Title
 591.9411'5

ISBN 0-575-04640-6

Photoset in Great Britain by
Rowland Phototypesetting Ltd, Bury St Edmunds, Suffolk
and printed by St Edmundsbury Press Ltd,
Bury St Edmunds, Suffolk